EMOTIONAL MEMORY

EMOTIONAL MEMORY

*Exploring
How Emotions
Impact Our Health*

Tina DeMatteo

PRAKASHA
Chicago, IL

Prakasha
Chicago, IL

Library of Congress Control Number: 2023919908

Paperback ISBN: 979-8-9888502-0-5
eBook ISBN: 979-8-9888502-1-2

The information contained in this book is for educational purposes only. All information is not in place of medical or psychological advice and is not meant to diagnose, treat, or cure any disease or mental health concern.

Book cover and interior design by Erin Seaward-Hiatt
Editorial production by kn literary

www.tinadematteo.com

CONTENTS

INTRODUCTION

A Healing Journey

HE SAID HE WOULD be home after work and we could finally talk about the tension that we had been going through that week. He came in and went straight to the bathroom. He then walked into the dining room where I was sitting and pulled up a chair to face me. He looked like he had been crying. He told me he had just met with an attorney and he wanted a divorce.

I was shocked and speechless. Not shocked that our struggles had led to a breakdown in our marriage, but it happened so suddenly that I didn't see it coming. I was speechless as to what to say to turn something so big around with words I failed to use through the years of our struggles.

I told him to let us break down this wall together so we could look back from the other side and see that we overcame this big challenge. I tried to reason with him by saying others who often make it to thirty years and beyond of marriage have once, too, faced divorce. I believed that we could work things out. He, on the other hand, said, "We tried, and this is a failed marriage." He lost hope. I said, "Walking away from problems cannot be an answer." He didn't even push back with a response and said that he was going to sleep over at a friend's house.

He left.

I buried my face in my hands and sobbed. I was not only losing the man I loved, but also his family. I was losing the holidays, birthday parties, vacations, and summer barbecues, all of which I had never had before him because I didn't have a close family. I knew the feeling of being alone and often on the verge of homelessness.

I always felt homeless since I was a child. After my mom left us, my grandmother, who owned the house we lived in, often said, "You better figure out what you're going to do, because I'm selling this house!" I was eleven. Where was I supposed to go? My father, like my mother, was an alcoholic, and there wasn't closeness between my siblings and me that would have helped us come together and figure something out.

The last I saw of my mother was her walking out the door, holding a paper bag in her arms, which probably contained only a few essentials, while leaving everything else behind. She left as if she were going to work that morning but never returned. My grandmother said she would take care of us, but she projected her unhappiness onto us. She and another family member took out their misery on us kids, as if everything that didn't go right in their lives was our fault.

One morning after my mother left us, my grandmother and I were standing by her bedroom dresser while she put her jewelry on. She said to me, "You know your mother left you because she didn't love you enough." I responded,

"I know," sadly. A child already interprets the loss of a parent as being their fault, but she certainly enforced it. Her continuous shaming through the years set me up for a lifetime of shame. I know now that my mother left an emotionally complicated marriage filled with emotional and physical abuse.

My mother became a serious alcoholic. It started to become a known problem after she fell down the stairs at a friend's house. She asked me to help her avoid drinking from that point forward. I used to go to her alcohol hiding places and pour some out. She also tried to kill herself twice (that I know of) with pills and asked me to keep an eye on her, but that everything would be okay, because she threw up the pills. We gardened and picked weeds to keep her moving.

My mother left my father two times before but took us with her. That was after we lived on a farm as a family, where my father kept horses. Something happened there between my parents, because we all moved back one year later to our old house in the city, and then my mother took us kids with her to another state, where her mother lived. The third and last time she left, I heard that her mother told her that it was too much to bring the children, so she left without us. I learned that she died about six years later. My father died a few years after her.

Through the years, the traumas layered on, and even though I didn't feel impacted, it showed in my behavior. I became a people pleaser while putting myself aside, most likely in hope that someone would like me. I did not have someone that could be a grounding adult force in my life and to help me through my emotional trauma.

I always felt that I was not good, likable, or lovable enough. Both my grandmother and other family members were sure to stress that, saying, "Who do you think you are?" and "Shut up, you don't know what you're talking about!" I struggled to make friends in school and always asked others if they were mad at me. (I go back and hug my younger self now.) I was a bit awkward, and people let me know it.

I had a crossed eye, which I was not born with. It developed as a result of the MMR vaccine that I received around two years old. I remember my mother showing me a picture and telling me that the entire right side of my face turned red, and my eye became inflamed and crossed. Both eyes would cross sometimes because the left eye was trying to see for the right eye. I was sensitive about the way I looked and was always looking down when I talked with people. My eyes are not crossed anymore. I balanced my health and my eyes became balanced, looking straight and forward.

Through the years, I strived to be the best student and worked hard to feel good enough. I was a straight-A student on the honor roll, the winner of spelling bees, and always took pride in my perfect attendance awards.

Two months before my mother left, she enrolled us in a new school. We went from a private Catholic school to a dilapidated neighborhood public school. Their curriculum was so behind the other school I had attended. They wanted to double promote me, but it didn't happen, so I inched my way toward graduation, very bored. I was accepted into a high school for children with higher grades, but I chose to go where my sister and brother went. Sadly, I quit just as they did. I felt that I had to quit so I could work to have my basic needs met. I later got my GED.

I worked hard through my teens and twenties, working odd jobs to make my way. It looked on the outside as if I had reached financial success, and others would come to me, asking me for money. I ended up hating money, and it showed in how I struggled financially in the years to come. I struggled to work at all because of my emotional safety issues and preferred to be alone. I developed a strong connection with the universe and never *felt* alone.

Universal awareness was all I had, as my family was not close. We were a very uneducated family that lived impoverished, with constant problems. My brother was on his own path. My sister and I would hang out, but we were further apart than it looked. We all shared one small bedroom in the back of the small shack that we lived in. As teenagers without adult guidance, we did not make the best choices. Our father was gone all day at the horse track as a horse trainer and came home drunk in the evening. Through the days and nights, I saw people coming in and out of our bedroom, engaging in activities of drugs and alcohol. My sister came home pregnant at sixteen and we were raising a baby as young teenagers. I would have never thought then that I would struggle to have my own children in my marriage.

My ex-husband and I struggled in very similar ways as I did in my childhood. We lived paycheck to paycheck. He was a dedicated worker at a job that he didn't like while I struggled to work at all. We occupied ourselves with emotional distractions. He was occupied with his calming beer, while I watched jarring news on a loop. Our issues became layered in distractions, and we lost connection to one another.

I always acknowledged that I had an addictive personality that showed in my distractions but learned that I did not like anything having an influence over me. I became disciplined early on so as not to engage in addictions such as alcohol, drugs, and cigarettes. I became extremely ill when I would drink alcohol and would vomit into the following evening.

Recovering from drinking just to feel healthy again became a waste of my time and energy. I questioned if I had alcoholic tendencies like my parents because I would have a second glass of wine. I didn't like having to ask the question and I wanted nothing to do with alcohol. I now understand that getting sick was based on a histamine response.

I look back at my childhood and see I always seemed to have histamine issues. I would wonder why my lips would look bigger than normal sometimes. Once, my mother asked the local pharmacist why my cheeks would get so red. He said that I was allergic to the sun and to wash my face with a special soap. Unbelievable.

I also always seemed to chase a dopamine high from caffeine or chocolate. I found myself doing it in secret because I was known to get really sick. Now, it is not even worth it. I know I get sick with migraines from drinking coffee or eating a food that doesn't agree with me. The health consequences are not worth coffee or a piece of chocolate to me.

I struggled through the years with food and chemical sensitivities, but people didn't believe me because the symptoms weren't always visible. I was sensitive to the smell of cigarette smoke, as it reminded me of my childhood but also gave me a headache. My ex-husband smoked for years, and I felt as if I were right back in my childhood home, where my mother and father both smoked in the house. I was considered pretentious by many because I did not engage in the big addictions and had a very healthy diet. They seemed to forget that both my parents were alcoholics and smokers who had died because of their vices. Why should this even be questioned? It wasn't clear to those who questioned my health choices, though, that I engaged in many other distractions that satisfied an addictive personality. I tried to distract myself from my ongoing struggles.

My ex-husband and I were both stressed, and we would trigger each other—not intentionally, but because our nervous systems were just stressed to the limit. Two people who have a lot of past traumas are not able to co-regulate each other and need a calming presence. I learned through all my healing and our continued friendship that we both did the best we knew how at the time.

I would have never believed our marriage to be an ending to what started when we were at a summer solstice celebration in 2005. He came to me and opened his hand to reveal two cherries from the bowl that the facilitator brought from her backyard tree. In my innocence, I chose one of the cherries from his hand and put it into his mouth. He then fed me the other. I thought to myself, "I think I just started something here." We walked along the path back to the car that we came together in—first as friends and then with potential for something more.

We met two days later at the lake and shared our feelings. We watched the full moon rise from the horizon, which led to a celebration every month going to the lake to do the same. The continuation of our relationship was a big deal for both of us, as our past relationships were known to not be solid or to last. We pledged to each other that we would move forward and no matter what happened, we would have no shame and no regret. That was kind of ironic because our relationship was filled with shame and regret. We struggled to figure out life together and we became stuck in our struggles.

I became pregnant three months into our relationship, and we planned to get married. For years, a baby was all I said that I wanted. I was excited and scared at the same time. He, on the other hand, was purely scared and was not happy about it. The stress I endured led to a loss at twelve weeks. I was devastated and became depressed. There was no room for progression in our relationship because we were both numb with pain from all our difficulties.

After two and a half years of struggle in our relationship, he went to visit someone in his extended family who hated me. He came back and told me that he wanted to split up. He told me that she said, among other awful things, "You need to leave Tina because she is never going to make anything of herself." They were the same words I had heard from my family growing up. This statement would shame me into depression for many years to come. I gave her so much power, but little did I know then that I would feel so grateful for the pain and embody a power now that cannot be found outside of us. I send her peace and love now.

He made up his mind that he was going to leave me and we were not getting married. I was overwhelmed with grief.

We got separate apartments.

I was so devastated from our separation that my mouth felt locked shut and I couldn't eat. I tried to take in broth and healthy soft fats, like avocados, but I lost twenty pounds, which I could not afford to lose being ninety pounds and four foot eleven. I went with a friend to a neighborhood vegetarian restaurant to talk and ate half of a veggie burger. I got home and noticed my lips looked like balloons and my throat was closing. I was having a serious histamine reaction to what I ate.

This would be the start of years of histamine issues. Everything I ate for the next year made my lips swell. I suffered serious acid reflux and broke out in hives. My emotional state was affecting my body profoundly. I understood that my health concerns were a reaction to my breakup relating to my abandonment issues from losing my mother as a child. At that point, I had done so much psychological work. I had taken psychology classes, done spiritual weekend retreats, and was well read on how our childhood traumas affect us.

I said to myself, "I worked through it all, so why am I in such a devastated state?" Well apparently, I didn't work through it all. It wasn't enough for me to just understand something psychologically and be free of future emotional obstacles. I knew I needed to work through every level of my being—physical, psychological, emotional, and spiritual. I knew I needed the experience of the breakup to heal my childhood trauma.

Our relationship never completely ended. We never stopped talking and he was over at my apartment so often that I gave him a key. A year and a half later, we decided to move back in together. We were married one month later, without working on any of our prior struggles. We wanted a child and we figured we would just go for it, although we had struggled through the years to have children.

I watched everyone around me have children. I heard sneering comments from others who didn't let me forget that I was not a mother. I would go to family Mother's Day parties that coincided with my birthday. I would feel very left out as I looked at family pictures that were clearly missing my child. People would ask, "Why aren't you pregnant yet?" Others would comment when I tried to give child or baby advice, saying, "Well, you're not a mom!" It affected me so profoundly that I started to feel that I was not worthy enough to be a mother. We never did have children and that is probably good, considering the outcome of our marriage.

I was under so much stress in our marriage. We struggled financially, as I failed to find work as an acupuncturist. I knew that change was needed and that I had to be the initiator. In 2014, I registered to go back to school to get a biology degree. That was important to me because I had to leave high school early to get a job to support myself and I was not able to get a formal college degree. I figured that I needed to make some kind of change and that was how I was going to do it. Although I felt at the time that it was the best decision I ever made in my life, the stress mounted even more with the demands of school.

I was feeling fatigued and had a blood test done. I was told over the phone (yes, over the phone) that it was very likely that I had bone marrow cancer. I dismissed it. I wanted nothing to do with a cancer diagnosis. The nurse said that the doctor wanted me to come back to the office for additional testing and not to search "Dr. Google" in the meantime. I did not go back. I knew I was under an extreme amount of stress and what was seen on the test was a result of my stress. I think I was more beside myself because of the unethical deliverance of something so dire said over the phone.

My stress was mounting, and I experienced more health symptoms. As an acupuncturist, I drew from my knowledge of nutrition and Chinese medicine and made certain not to consume any food that would cause inflammation. I brought balance to the imbalances. I took my focus off it all as a problem and focused on my internal health as a whole. The symptoms subsided.

It is now over a decade later and I am very healthy. Fear takes us down. We get a diagnosis, which brings on fear and often leads to death. I never told my ex-husband or anyone else of my health concerns because I didn't want their emotions on my health. I knew what I needed to do, and I did not have to look outside of myself for answers.

I took care of my health and kept on with my classes while I could feel my husband moving further and further away, and every time I came up with a plan to help us, he was against it. I felt that I was constantly up against opposition. I wanted to move because our upstairs neighbor, who worked the night shift, kept me up all night when she was home and pounded on her floor if I even made a small noise during the day or if my ex-husband dared to talk. I was losing sleep and it affected my health and marriage. She traumatized me. When I did move, if I heard a noise from a neighbor, I would jump, so I started using a fan as white noise. I told myself that I couldn't live in an apartment anymore. It was extremely unhealthy for me.

My ex-husband didn't want to move. He liked our apartment. We had a nice place on a lake with a balcony facing the water and we watched the sunrise every morning. I kept telling him that it didn't matter how nice a place was if it affected our health and marriage. We were clearly not working together to advance our goals.

Years earlier, when we moved back in together and wanted a child, we did so without working on our previous issues, as if they had gone away. Our love for each other was not enough to break through our life obstacles. We were two people who were emotionally down and struggled to lift each other up. Seven years later, we became another statistic and divorced.

I seemed to have no say in my divorce. It went so fast and there were many people sharing their opinions with him that were not in my favor. I said that I would not go through what I did last time with my swelling lips and overall health. I knew I needed to take extra care of myself. I was a vegetarian for about twenty-seven years, but I started eating chicken for a while so I could make the broth for healing.

The main reason I gave up meat in the past was because I used to get sick from it, which was apparently my histamine issue. I started making chicken broth and would freeze the remaining amount immediately to minimize bacteria production, which can result in a histamine reaction. I also learned that when I ate gluten or dairy, my lips swelled, and I felt as if I was having a panic attack. I removed all gluten and dairy from my diet as well.

I stayed with a few friends who offered to take me in while my divorce was underway. I learned that these relationships were also unhealthy for me, and I needed to purge them all from my life. My first stay was in a neighboring state with an old friend, where I learned that distance would not make my problems go away. After two weeks of shaming comments and emotional unrest, I rented a car and went back to my neighborhood, only a few blocks from the home that I had lived in with my ex-husband.

It was fascinating to watch the behaviors of others whom I no longer needed to keep me in unhealthy emotional patterns for the false security of familiarity. I was called crazy for wanting to retreat to my room while I was going through my divorce, weird for following the diet that I did, and strange for going to bed early and waking up early. I was told that my divorce was entirely *my* fault. I was asked, "How can you have let this happen?" and then was told by several different people to "get over it!"

My divorce was so timely, set right before Thanksgiving. I was trying to work through my emotions of the death of my marriage and family. I had three final exams coming up. I said to the girl I was staying with, "I am so overwhelmed!" I was told in response, "I think it's your age." I was later told that I should go on a date and go dancing.

The day after my divorce was finalized, the friend who I was staying with asked me to go for a walk. She said that I was acting rigid and told me that I should try to lighten up. I said, "Do you remember what happened yesterday?" She said, "Yeah, but can you at least try?" As if just being quiet was a bother to her. She went on to tell me that I was going to need to move soon because her sister was moving in. The struggles kept rolling in.

I felt so much gratitude for those who helped me in such a painful time, but I struggled with the comments because I grew up with shaming comments. I know deep down that we all struggle to say the right things at difficult moments; it's just hard to hear when we're in pain.

I finally got my own apartment a year and a half after my divorce, which was my fifth move after leaving my home. I was writing a lot by then; suddenly I felt it come through me so fast. I was writing e-books in short amounts of time. The words were flying through my fingers onto the keyboard. I was still busy taking biology classes while doing constant research for my writing in my off time. I was on a mission to get my message of how our emotions impact our health into the world.

A year after I moved into my apartment, I faced eviction. I struggled with finding work, again. I put an extreme amount of effort in all day to find work. I would lie down to go to sleep at night, and as I went over my day, I knew I did everything to propel myself forward with finding work. I was left so confused. I finally learned and realized that it was not because I was doing something wrong or that I was not good enough; it was that as an acupuncturist, I was trying to work one-on-one with strangers when I had serious emotional safety issues from my past traumas. I was not in alignment with what I was trying to do for work.

With everything I had going on, I still felt completely on purpose with my writing and so connected to the universe. The synchronistic events that kept happening to my benefit had me feeling completely held by the universe.

However, I felt misunderstood, judged, and held back by one last longtime friend. She clearly did not want to see me rise up and tried everything to keep me down. She showed that she felt threatened by the passion I was showing for my work. I asked her for help in reading some e-books that I was going to put on my website and I didn't hear from her for a month, which was unusual. That happened twice. Years of manipulation to hold me back from rising up came to light and I finally let her go from my life. I vowed that I would only have friends in my life who were authentic, believed in me, and wanted to see me rise up. After I got off the phone from telling her that I needed time to be by myself with no outside influence, I had a flash vision of my grandmother. I saw it as resolving generations of unresolved emotional memory.

With no outside influence from anyone, I started to feel an even deeper connection with the universe. I felt a deep gratitude for a depth of knowing that could not be denied. I knew that I had to stop fighting what was seemingly inevitable and that I was safe, and everything would be okay. I said to the universe, "Okay, I hear you." I surrendered to this deep knowing and felt so filled with gratitude that it brought tears to my eyes. I felt one with everything. I felt one with the birds, bees, flowers, and trees, with the clouds above and mycelium below. It was beautiful.

I managed to get a sublet apartment for five months, but I knew when the five months were up, it was likely that I would have nowhere to go. I finished my spring semester and painfully learned I had reached the limit of my student loans. I was not going to be able to finish my biology degree. I went to the financial aid office to apply for a scholarship because I was a candidate with my straight As that I had proudly earned. They told me that I needed to come back to apply in a couple of months. Only a couple of months from then would reveal more obstacles.

I knew it was likely that I would be homeless at the end of my sublease, so I continued to look for a shared apartment again. I had money to pay for it. I hoped for a place that would not be as constantly noisy as the current one, which was overwhelming. I also hoped for a garden that would help ground me through the emotional times I was going through. I knew that sharing an apartment with a roommate meant sharing beliefs and values that might end up being different than mine and probably wouldn't work out, but I continued to look and apply.

I did not have much in belongings but found myself getting rid of memorable things that I never thought I would. I was poised to release every last material possession from my life. I felt no restriction in getting rid of my things. I was so filled with gratitude for everything that I felt that lined up for me at that point. It was a love that no person or material possession could match.

The day had come, and I needed to leave. I had a bag to carry a few essentials, my computer, and a water bottle.

I left the keys for my apartment under the door and walked into the wild.

I had a plan to go to a neighboring suburb that I considered safer than the area where I lived, but the days and weeks to come proved to be more difficult than I had planned. I learned when the businesses close at night that the streets become alive with people with nowhere to go. I usually go to sleep really early when I have a home and do not even feel safe to go out in the dark. However, in the five weeks that I was outside, I felt completely safe and held by the universe. It felt as if I had bodyguards surrounding me.

I dealt with temperature fluctuations. It was thirty-eight degrees one night in June, which is usually warmer in the Northwest at that time of year. On the second day I was outside, it poured rain so hard. I stood under an awning for the entire night, watching the rain come down in sheets. I put a plastic bag over my computer bag to protect it. I couldn't lose my computer because I needed it for my writing. That experience changed my actions as to what I would do in extreme weather in the weeks to come. I chose to rent a car two times for the weeks that it was supposed to rain. At least I was sheltered in a car and was able to get a little sleep. I had money. My bills were paid. I even bought a six-hundred-dollar gift card to Whole Foods, so I knew I had money set aside to have food every day. Homelessness is not about money. It is not about lazy people who do not want to work. There is deeper unresolved emotional pain that needs healing. I knew it was up to me to see where I needed healing and to take action.

I did not feel a victim of my circumstance—I felt blessed to have tapped into my passion for writing. I felt like I was on a mission to achieve my writing goals and had purpose for living.

I was feeling connected to everyone and everything and found myself giving money to other homeless people who had no idea I was one of them. I walked down the street with a smile on my face just happy to be on purpose. One day I gave money to this homeless man I would see every day on my way to get lunch. He was artsy-looking with dreadlocks and had such a loving presence about him. As I gave him the little cash that I had in my pocket, I said to him, "You know, you can end this today—you have the power within." He replied, "I know, I know," nodding his head in agreement. I don't know what made me say those words. They were probably the words I personally needed to hear. I never did see him again. Hopefully I helped him.

I had all confidence that life would change for me if I stayed on purpose. Although I was extremely sleep deprived, I went to a coffee shop every morning to use the internet. I bought a green tea as my ticket to spend the entire day there. I am not one for loud music and people all around me, but I persevered and kept writing. I was making progress.

I have always been a very private person, but one day I shared my story with a woman who was a frequent customer at the coffee shop. She shared pieces of information that alluded to her once experiencing something similar. When I saw her again, she kept her distance from me. I knew right away she was staying away from me. I had triggered something in her emotionally.

A couple of weeks later, I saw her again and she was not very nice and expressed it cruelly. As she spoke, her voice faded into the background as I told myself what she was saying was not about me but about her past homeless issues. I left and held back my tears so I would not make a spectacle of myself while I walked down the street.

I looked up to the sky and boldly said, "*This ends today!*"

I also stated emphatically what was important for me to have: a home, nourishing organic food, and relationships with those who believe in me and the work that I was doing. It was most important to me that I felt I was believed in.

My homelessness did end that day and the beginning of a magnificent life began. I ran into an old friend the following morning who I had not seen in many years. He gave me a place to stay, and we became the closest of friends. I had never felt so seen and understood in my entire life.

A couple of weeks later, I was emotionally triggered again, and the energy went right up into my eyes. I lost my vision!

It was similar to what had happened six months earlier. I was under an enormous amount of stress and had a kaleidoscope headache with flashing lights in my visual field. Everything went black except for my nerves being lit up in the background. I took a high dose of magnesium to calm my nerves, did acupuncture, and woke up with vision. This time it was different. I saw the flashes of light at first, but for the following week, my vision was clouded from the pressure in my eyes and I saw bright light.

We can get so caught up in our emotions that we aren't able to see past them. I stewed in my emotional pain for three days as I vomited and my head felt as if it was going to split open. My eyes were blood red, inflamed, and angry looking. My body attempted to discharge the energy and reset my nervous system through uncontrollable shaking and trembling, but it did not release the pressure from my eyes. I learned so much from that entire experience that it helped me to prevent a future response one year later.

I realized that my vision loss was more serious than I thought and that I needed to go to the emergency room. My friend drove me to and from the hospital for several days. The doctors labeled me with glaucoma and made comments that they felt it was unlikely my vision would return. I did not believe it. I stood in the office and prayed.

I said to the universe, "I need to get my vision back. I did not go through all the pain in my life to not be able to share it in my writing!" Although, I then thought optimistically that I could use audio if my vision did not return. I said at that moment that I would do everything possible to help as many people as I could with my work.

My living situation had me limited in what I would do for healing if I were in a more secure place. I needed magnesium to help me calm down my nervous system. I was still trying to heal from my sleep deprivation from the weeks of homelessness and I had been drinking too much green tea, both of which dilate the eyes.

The doctors would not hear my story of what led up to the episode. They were focused on my eyes as separate from the rest of my body. The pressure in my eyes was at 62 millimeters of mercury (mmHg). The normal range is anywhere from 10–21 mmHg. After numerous attempts to lower the pressure, zapping my eyes with a laser and sticking needles in to extract fluid, they told me that the only way to save my vision was to do surgery to release the pressure. I felt the weight of being a burden to my friend who had just run into me a few weeks earlier. Without vision, I was suddenly going to be his responsibility. I felt the pressure.

I went along with it, and subsequent tests showed that I had no damage to my retinas or optic nerves. The doctors told me that I was lucky. One doctor said that 98 percent of people with what I had would not be walking in his office freely without a guide. I don't believe I was lucky. I believe that I healed from the power within myself even though they did the surgery. It is fascinating that with pressure at 62 mmHg that there was no damage.

I believe I would have been able to naturally get my vision back, like I did six months prior, or not have had it go as far if I was in a different situation. I have had health concerns over the years that tied back to the first time my lips swelled. I healed myself every time by dismissing it and not becoming one with it. I even ended my homeless issue with a bold statement. I somehow allowed myself to become one with the vision issue though. I accepted it. It is a strange acceptance, as if only to know that I could get through it, because I have been through so much before. The magnitude of the emotional trigger clouded what I came to know with my recent opening to truth.

We become stronger from our pain. I am now grateful for my health challenges because I can help others with what I went through. I am also very aware of all the health concerns that arise from emotional pain that has not been worked through, as explained in the Adverse Childhood Experiences (ACE) Study in chapter 2. I have a jarring complete score of ten from the ACE's questionnaire, but I plan to live a long and healthy life. I feel empowered by my knowledge and am healthier because of it. I transformed my emotions, and I can stand grounded in calm in challenging times.

When I was younger, I had an out-of-body experience that showed me what I already understood: that we are more than our physical bodies. I thought I was dying as my soul left my physical body and hovered above me at the ceiling. I was in awe of the visual images that came to me prior to leaving my body. There was a lot of uncertainty involved for me though, despite being very aware of these types of experiences.

To know that we are not only our body and mind helps us to know that we do not have to suffer in our emotional experiences. We get stuck in our struggles that lead us to suffering. We can end our emotional pain and live a healthy and happy life.

The devastation from my divorce and the many traumas in my life led me down a healing path that would expand my heart. I learned that so many obstacles in my life were blessings in disguise. I now see that it was me that was fighting against myself. I also see that not finishing my formal education degrees was a blessing because I never got caught in the conditioning of the education system. The universe seemed to always be by my side, even though I fought against it. I will not fight against the universe or myself anymore. I live free.

I want to share my knowledge to help heal the emotional traumas of everyone out there who struggles with navigating through their emotional pain. We all have the innate ability to heal and to be free of suffering. We have the ability to create wonderful and lasting positive changes in our lives. I did and am still in awe when I recount all my blessings.

I live in a house now with no traumatizing banging, a beautiful garden that I created, and I am healthy and in peace. We will inevitably go through emotional challenges through life, but we do not have to suffer. We have a choice. I choose peace—how about you?

How This Book Is Structured

This book is divided into three parts: Part I: How Our Emotions Impact Our Health; Part II: How Our Health Impacts Our Emotions; and Part III: Emotional Transformation: An Exploration to Transcend Emotional Pain. The first two parts unveil the science behind our emotions and how our emotions can affect our health and how our health can further affect our emotions. The last part explores our behavior to transform our emotional pain. It focuses on basic awareness of our everyday lives to help us to step out of the control and conditioning of society and learn to discern truth for ourselves.

What You'll Find Inside

The chapters that follow offer the information we need to heal on all levels of our being. We cannot only try to heal in one area and expect complete health. We also cannot succumb to saying that we have tried everything and nothing worked, therefore giving up and staying in an unhealthy and unhappy state. My hope is to empower every reader with the fact that we all have the innate ability to heal and we need to persevere.

Parts I and II focus on how our emotions, diet, and lifestyle can affect our health and then further affect our emotions. Part I focuses on how our past emotional traumas and experiences can lead to health concerns. I include statistical data as well as other scientific findings to back up my writing. I encourage everyone to read all cited information to get a larger view of what is not made available from the mainstream media or our education system.

Emotional memory is a term I use that can be defined as our unresolved emotions that are kept stored in their fragmented state. We express our emotions through that fragmented memory, so we need to heal our unresolved emotions to heal all parts of our being. Memory is always trying to balance out, but it needs our participation.

I refer to the memory of our individual minds as the memory that we all associate with to recall past experiences that are specific to this lifetime. I write about the memory of our personal being that can be related to the karma of our body, or our soul, or spirit that is part of who we are in all lifetimes. Finally, I write about the collective memory we share that connects all individual memory beings as one memory.

Hindu philosophies speak of karma from our past. As Swami Sarvapriyananda from the Vedanta Society of New York says, "The accumulated impressions of past lives are in the subtle body, and they go on from lifetime to lifetime. Physical bodies die and subtle bodies go on."[1]

Karma is often believed to bring justice to a wrongdoing, but we can instead look at karma to be balancing the memory of our being. We can look at the emotional memory of our being as the accumulated impressions from our emotional experiences. However, memory is memory.

Ending emotional attachments comes up a lot through this book. It is in our emotional attachments where suffering exists. Our suffering has nothing to do with the object to which we are attached. It is the feeling within us that seeks the object of our desire that we think will fulfill a feeling of lack. Ending emotional attachments does not mean to be cold or aloof or to end relationships; it is to be able to stand completely in peace if we were to lose the attached.

I use the words *truth, awareness, light, the true nature of our being,* and *consciousness* interchangeably. I often use *awareness* to explain being aware of our surroundings. *Shared awareness* refers to the pure conscious awareness that we are all a part of. You can discern for yourself the meaning needed for your personal healing.

Part II focuses on how our current health concerns lead to emotional pain that keeps us in a loop of chronic illness. My hope is that the information I share will inspire you to take the initiative to be in control of your own health to live a life of balance and peace.

Finally, in Part III, I try to bring to light the different behaviors we share as a collective that lead us to suffering. I am aware that not everyone feels physical pain in their emotional suffering. I personally felt physical pain as constriction in my chest, as if my heart were truly breaking. I also experienced intense headaches that were directly correlated to my emotional suffering. For the context of this book, *pain* and *suffering* are used interchangeably, but do know that, no matter the term, if we are not in peace and we struggle in life, then we are in suffering.

This is not a book with steps or methods to follow for healing. This book points out how we all act through our emotions, and it is up to you to discern for yourself what resonates and how to apply the information. It is in the recognition of what needs healing that we are opened to further exploring healing and integrating it into life.

This is not work that can be skimmed through. Transforming our emotional pain requires time and dedication. Even when we recognize the true nature of our being or are liberated from suffering, we must shed old conditioning. I believe that the first two parts of this book are critical in the emotional transformation process, because we must be aware of everything that contributes to our emotional health. We are physical, emotional, spiritual, and psychological beings, and we must address all areas of health to completely heal.

We all have the innate ability to heal. We do not have to go through crises like I did to understand this truth. Sadly, we often wait until catastrophes happen to nudge us forward. I say that we all take the initiative to do the healing work so we can be healthier and happier personally and express that into the collective.

I started my healing journey inquiring as to why two people who love each other cannot figure out how to make a relationship last. I never followed any particular path of spirituality and opened up to this knowledge as I opened to truth. I learned a lot and I healed. Now, I want to share my work with all who have struggled with their emotions and suffer.

I am teaching through the lens of an acupuncturist, registered herbalist, and through my biology education, but most of all through my life experience. I am the first to say that it is not easy to transform our emotions, but the beauty, peace, and freedom that are seen and felt on the other side of our pain are enough for me to say that it is worth it to persevere.

Our work is never done. We do not reach a peak of emotional or spiritual enlightenment. We must be willing to constantly do the work so we can enjoy good health, healthy relationships, and share the love of who we are with the entire collective. My hope is that you will join me on this healing journey to stand healthy and in peace.

Light, love, peace, and healing to all.

PART I

How Our Emotions Impact Our Health

CHAPTER 1

Emotional Memory

WE ARE ABOUT TO be enlightened to the fact that memory is not limited to the brain of a biological being. We will know with clarity at the end of this book how our unresolved emotional memories impact our health, relationships, and the collective. Our health and life struggles will be seen as fragmented memory that can indeed be balanced. To heal our health is to heal our emotional pain.

We all have childhood or other emotional traumas of which the memories can be haunting. These memories remain with us whether we are aware of them or not. Memories are held as a resonant frequency pattern throughout our being. We see our unresolved emotional pain manifest as life struggles and health concerns until we are aware that we can end our suffering.

We are a traumatized society that suffers individually and collectively. According to the National Institute of Mental Health (NIMH), an estimated twenty-one million adults in the United States in 2020 had at least one major depressive episode.[1] Our emotions are easily influenced by societal events. We heal when we take control of our emotional health.

Living with the memories of unresolved emotional pain has an effect on our health. It is our emotional memories that drive our behaviors in diet and lifestyle. Our health is dependent on the healing of our emotional pain. Our memories will not go away with medication, nor can they be erased. Our imbalanced emotions are expressed as health concerns over time.

The Centers for Disease Control and Prevention (CDC) state that approximately two million new cancer cases were reported in 2019,[2] while obesity prevalence was 41.9 percent from 2017–2020.[3] These health concerns do not just appear one day but were absent the previous day. Could our health concerns be born from unresolved emotional memories?

Memories are a feedback process. Our beings remember memories, even if our minds forget. We act out the frequency of memories that we are in resonance with. The activities of our lives are the result of all memory coming through our being, which shows our alignment to the memory. It is our fragmented, unresolved emotional memories that keep us in a loop of suffering.

Our emotional memories not only affect our personal lives, but also those of the collective. We all contribute to the collective memory and connect with the memories that we align with through the frequency that we are. Our emotional memories have the ability to impact others and ourselves far more than we know.

Fragmented memory heals as we heal our unresolved emotions. Our unresolved emotions may be hidden from view but can be clearly seen in our personality and daily activities. Our health and life struggles come into balance as memory is brought into balance. Life is easier when we are not fighting against others or ourselves. We live without suffering. We live in peace.

We are limitless beings of memory in form. Healing our pain heals our health and our relationships and extends our peace into the collective. Suffering is our fragmented unresolved emotional memory manifest as emotional attachments. Our peace lies in the healing of our memory. We are a microcosm of the macrocosm. The healing of one is the healing of all.

What Is Emotional Memory?

We take for truth that emotions are transient. Many people confuse feelings for emotions, and the belief is accepted without reason. Memory is believed to only be what we remember from our past while not making the connection that all emotions are stored as memory. To heal our emotional pain is to expand our perception and see beyond what we already know.

Memory is memory, but emotional memory can be defined as our unresolved emotions that are kept stored in their fragmented state. We express our emotions though that fragmented memory, so the healing of our unresolved emotions is to heal all parts of our being. Memory is always trying to balance out, but it needs our participation. Healing memory leads to peace.

Emotions are often confused with feelings but are not the same. Emotions are an *expression* of our feelings and thoughts. Feelings are feedback from information we receive from our surroundings, as well as our personal memory and the memory of the collective. We use our senses to connect with our surrounding environment while always transmitting and receiving information with the field that we are a part of. Our feelings ignite our emotions.

Emotions are activated from the release of physiological neurotransmitters.[4] We believe that emotions are transitory, as we forget insignificant emotional moments but remember the intensity of others. An emotion may be brief based on the neurochemicals involved and our experience, but they stay encoded in memory. Our memories are forever, even if we forget them.

Every emotion we have is stored in the memory of our being and as collective memory. All emotions and traumas are imprinted as memory on every scale of our being. Our emotional memories are also stored in the collective and we have access to all memories, not just our own. We connect with emotional memories as the frequency that we are.

Emotions are frequencies that are stored as memory. Our emotional memories are held as a resonant frequency pattern of balance or imbalance. We connect with emotional memories through similarity as we align with another resonant frequency. Emotions are activated in our alignment with memory and reflect the frequency we are in *that* moment.

The balance or imbalance of our emotional frequency is seen in our health, relationships, and work lives. We attach to frequencies that feel familiar in our attempt to attain emotional security. Our unresolved emotional pain stays in a resonant holding pattern until we end our attachment. It is in our emotional attachment that we are living with a false sense of security.

Emotions are a significant guide for the health of our being. We see where healing is needed through our emotional memories. We feel restriction in our body that corresponds to our unresolved pain. In our awareness, we see how we respond to our memories and know in depth what is needed for balance. Our emotional memories will show us the way.

Emotional memory is forever, even in the absence of visual memory. In our awareness, we can feel into our memories and know at the depth of our being the healing we need. It is in our alignment with the frequency of truth that we heal. Our unresolved emotional pain dissolves and the resonant frequency of our emotional memories transforms.

Fragmented Resonant Memory

Can we truly heal our emotional pain? We live with the pain of our past traumas and accept our life struggles as an inevitable result. Our painful memories reside as fragmented memory in and around our being. The imbalanced frequency stays locked in as resonant memory. Our emotional memories remain fragmented until we transform our resonance to balance.

Fragmented resonant memory holds our painful life stories. We see this fragmentation as health and other life struggles. Our body expresses physical imbalance where our emotions have resonated with an emotional event. The frequency of our fragmented memory remains until we become aware that we have the power to transform fragmentation into balanced memory.

Unresolved emotional memories resonate as an imbalance of frequency. We live out of alignment with the natural frequency that we are, and it shows in our emotional expressions.

We get emotionally activated when we hold unresolved emotional pain. It is in our awareness that we see our emotions as frequency of balance or imbalance.

The imbalance of frequency gets stuck in a fragmented resonant pattern. We avoid uncomfortable feelings and our being continues to relive painful memories of our past. We stay emotionally attached to childhood, ancestral, and collective trauma and live through the fragmentation of our resonant memory. We live a life of struggle, and it affects our health.

Fragmented resonant memory shows in specific areas. Our memories live within us and around the field of our being. We see fragmented memory expressed in areas of our bodies, as well as specific areas of our lives in correlation to past events. Our health and life struggles show us where healing is needed. It is in our awareness that we heal.

In our awareness, we see the truth of the frequency of our emotional pain. We know with depth that it is in a fragmented resonant holding pattern. We are aware that our pain stays alive as long as we stay emotionally attached. It is in our truth that we know we have the power to transform our fragmented resonant memories.

We are in resonance with the memories that we remember. The memories that we resonate with are at the frequency of our being in that moment in time. Troubling emotional memories are sharp indicators of fragmented resonance that needs to be balanced. We heal our memory when we heal our emotions.

Healing our emotional pain transforms us at the depth of our being. Our painful emotional memories may be stored fragmented but can be transformed into balance. We heal lifetimes of pain and struggle and extend our healing into the collective. We contribute to the healing of the collective mind. Our healing is healing for all.

Our emotional pain *can* be healed. Our memories can be transformed to resonate balance. In our transformation, we feel freedom as peace. We feel free of the burden of emotional pain and live a life that flows. It is in our balanced memories that we see truth. We transform fragmentation and our memories resonate as truth.

Collective Emotional Memory

We live with the memories of wars, pandemics, and other historical traumas. Our collective emotional memory is fragmented, and we all feel the impact. We see conflict and suffering in our personal lives and all around us. Our individual minds have an effect on our health and the health of the collective. Healing our personal memory heals collective memory.

Collective memory holds all emotional memory. We may all have individual minds, but the content is there for all to access. It is our resonant frequency that aligns with similar minds and memory. More people experiencing similar emotions strengthens the balance or imbalance of the collective emotional memory. Our individual minds are part of one collective mind.

In his scientific paper "Extended Mind, Power, & Prayer," Dr. Rupert Sheldrake suggests, "Our minds, in fact, may be vast, far-reaching spatially extended networks of connection."[5] In his hypothesis of formative causation, Sheldrake proposes that memory is inherent in nature and most of the so-called laws of nature are more like habits. He explains, "Each individual both draws upon and contributes to the collective memory."[6] We are individual minds sharing one conscious mind.

We all share the collective memory of societal traumas. The frequency is fixed into the collective memory and we feel it, even if we do not experience the traumas directly. Our emotions and reactions help to keep a narrative in a fragmented state or in balance. It is in our power to heal our emotions to balance our memory and share peace with the collective.

Our imbalanced emotions impact our health and become a part of the collective memory. Is it only a coincidence that society shares so many of the same health concerns while we share similar emotions? Those with similar emotional patterns tend to have similar behaviors, which in turn lead to specific health concerns. Emotional patterns lead to health patterns.

Healing is a challenge in a society filled with disorder. We see conflict and suffering where peace and order are needed. Our personal conflict and suffering affect the memory of the collective. It is in our personal peace and order that we contribute peace and order. We are all part of the collective mind with an influence on the collective memory far greater than we know.

Our unresolved emotions affect the frequency of our being, and its fragmented pattern of memory is shared with the collective mind. Our thoughts not only affect the balance of our being, our relationships, and local community, but they have an effect across the entire universe. There is a deep responsibility in this knowing.

The healing of our collective emotional memory begins with our personal healing. We heal our personal fragmented memory through balancing our emotions. In our healing, we feel peace. In our peace, we contribute our balanced frequency into the collective. The transformation of unresolved memory shows as order all around us.

There is a lot of suffering stored in our collective memory. We see generations of struggle in our personal lifetimes and the memories can be recurrent. It is the frequency of our being from our emotions that keeps us tied to memories. We cannot make memories go away, but we have the power to stand in peace in the face of troubling memories.

Collective memory is forever. Balancing our personal memory transforms our relation to it. We are settled in calm and are not reactive to the disruptions to our ever-changing world. We see clearly that peace is the true nature of our being and we do not go against others or ourselves. We live in peace as unified memory.

CHAPTER 2

Memory Expressed

O UR EMOTIONAL MEMORIES DO indeed affect our health. We live with unresolved trauma, without being aware that it fragments our resonance and can be expressed through our health. We see others with similar health concerns as ours but do not see a connection as an emotional alignment. Expressed emotions are significant indicators to the health of our being.

All health concerns that are visible or hidden from view were born from a previous cause. We see memory expressed as emerging health concerns that seem to come out of nowhere, but emotional memory lies in waiting until activated. Trauma fragments the resonance of our being and stays in that resonant pattern until we balance the fragmentation.

Our health concerns are too often narrowed down to genetics and unknown causes. We are labeled with diseases from a list of symptoms and then told they are related to genetics with nothing that can be done. It seems plausible to instead see similar family health concerns connected to similar emotional patterns. Emotions can be transformed, and our health healed.

The emotional memories of our past can lead to serious health concerns. From 1995 to 1997, Kaiser Permanente and the CDC collaborated on the infamous Adverse Childhood Experiences (ACE) Study.[1] There were 17,337 participants in the study. The goal was to determine if traumatizing events in childhood led to health concerns later in life. They found that when trauma gets activated, it can lead to many diseases, including chronic lung, heart, and autoimmune diseases and cancer, as well as struggles with addiction. We heal our physical bodies when we transform our emotional pain.

We can learn a lot from individuals or groups with similar emotional patterns. It is interesting that there are people who share similar life struggles and health concerns. Can it be pure coincidence that we come across others with the same health concerns or look back to encounters of the past that correlate to our current health? It makes sense that we are or were in alignment with the frequency of these individuals.

Awareness of our fragmented frequency can lead to healing. New technologies may emerge that can heal the frequency of our being, but our emotional healing work is vital to prevent regressing into our fragmented patterns. In our regression, health concerns we believe to be healed reappear. We can use technologies as assistance, but healing is in our innate power.

Health concerns do not have to be inevitable after experiencing trauma. If we transform our emotional pain from the point of trauma, we can end the potential for autoimmune and other health concerns to develop. Healing our emotional pain prevents an emotional activation from occurring in the future. We can live healthier lives, free of suffering.

Emotional memories can be transformed to balance. In our balance, we see our unresolved trauma for the truth that it is. We see common family health concerns as emotional memories that are in a similar fragmented pattern. We live in our awareness and see similar health concerns in others as a guide to what we may need to see. In our emotional transformation, we heal our health.

Emotional Memory Patterns

Our health can be seen in the emotional patterns of our lives. We see similar health concerns in our family. We connect with others who have similar struggles in health. Our health is an expression of the frequency of our being and our emotional patterns show through our behaviors. It is through our emotional memory patterns that we see where healing is needed.

We accept health struggles without looking for deeper reasons why they appear. Our emotional memories can be painful, so we avoid them. If we look, we can see patterns in our health correlated to specific experiences or life struggles. It is in the avoidance of our emotions that we see our memories come through as health patterns.

We see similar health struggles in our family that are considered to only be genetic. We take on the patterns of our parents and other significant figures in our lives. We are a reverberation of our parents from birth and have all previous generations of memory within us. It seems reasonable to see a connection between family health and emotional patterns.

Emotional memory patterns are seen in our connections with others. We resonate with others who have similar life and health struggles and can see similar patterns and cycles that are in opposition to other groups of individuals. Our personal relationships and others we encounter with similar health concerns can shine light on our fragmented emotional patterns.

Health patterns are in alignment with emotional memory patterns. Is it a coincidence that we see similar health concerns arise at specific emotional times in our lives? It is common to experience digestive concerns before an important event and a viral or autoimmune flare-up at a critical emotional stage in life. Health is an expression of our emotions.

Our emotional memory patterns show the frequency that we are. Our personality, behaviors, and lifetime troubles are indicators of our resonant memory patterns. Our health concerns grip us at the depth of our being and further affect our emotions. To heal our health is to heal our unresolved emotions. Balanced emotional memory leads to peace.

Health concerns of any kind equal fragmented memory. Our unresolved emotional memories express through our health patterns until we transform the resonant memory. Our action is needed to transform our pain. In our awareness, we make the connection to our health and emotional patterns. We bring order to fragmentation.

There is meaning in the health and emotional patterns of our lives. The messages continue to get louder until we are open to listening. It is in our emotional transformation that we can live a life without struggle. We meet our pain as it comes because we know that we will be free. It is in the freedom from our emotional pain that we live healthy and in peace.

To see our health expressed in balance is to have healed our emotional memory. In our balance, we live aware of the correlation between our health and emotional patterns. Our family and other connections become lights into the patterns that help us on our healing journey. We see our health patterns as an expression of our frequency. We see clearly how to heal.

Emotional Memory Activated

A traumatic event occurs and we become traumatized. The experience was painful, so we avoid the memories. Our emotional memory fragments. We numb our pain and accept life with all its troubles. We live attached to what we think is giving us comfort until we lose the attached and suffer in our loss. Our emotional memory gets activated.

Our initial traumatic experience gets stored in a fragmented memory pattern. We layer on more traumas through life, but the initial fragmentation stays in its pattern until a similar experience activates the memory. It can take many years from the initial trauma to get activated, and years after the activation to see our unresolved emotions turn to health symptoms.

More studies are being conducted to find a link between stress and illness. In fact, a recent Swedish cohort study was conducted that included 106,464 patients with stress-related disorders. It concluded that exposure to a stress-related disorder was significantly associated with increased risk of subsequent autoimmune disease.[2] To see the link is to prevent future illness.

We live in the avoidance of our painful memories. In our avoidance, we see our lives as difficult and live out the same emotional patterns. We relive our traumas through our relationships and life experiences as we cleverly choose what will shine light on our pain, and then we wait. We become complacent with the way things are.

Our pain grows along with our troubles. We distract and numb our pain with diet and lifestyle choices. We see patterns in our health and life struggles pointing to our emotional memory being activated. We ignore the signs only for them to get louder. In our fear, we hold on tighter. We live attached to our perceived comfort until we lose the attached.

In the loss of our emotional attachments, our emotional memories get activated. We may be aware of our struggles relating back to a significant event in life, but we stay in our pain. It is in our suffering that we see our symptoms grow and we subsequently get diagnosed with a serious illness. Our emotions affect our health and we see our health affect our emotions.

Emotional memory can be healed. To wait for our pain to go away leads to painful health struggles. Our balanced health is in the healing of our trauma *before* it has a chance to be activated. We suffer more in our avoidance. It is in our avoidance that our health declines slowly and we accept illnesses as age-related. We are powerful individuals with the power to heal.

We all have fragmented emotional memories that need healing. We can see our memories play out in our health and life struggles. We see our emotional memories get activated and our health get affected. Our health is dependent on our initiative to heal. It is in our healing that we live a life of freedom. We live free of emotional suffering.

Traumas occur, but true healing is possible. In our healing, we face our pain for the truth that it is to end our suffering.

To live in avoidance of our trauma is to hold on to our pain. Our pain stays with us as fragmented memory and ignites health concerns. We bring order to our fragmented memory when we balance our emotional memories.

Emotional Memory in Resonance

We can learn from similarity. Could it be that those who share similar forms also share similar health concerns? Can similar personalities, mannerisms, and traits be indicative of similar life struggles? Are we in resonance with people who express similar emotional patterns of behavior? Our forms and emotional patterns are indicators of our shared memory in resonance.

Our emotional memories come from how we have learned to express our emotions. We express ourselves as the frequency that we are. We take on emotional behaviors that are similar to our family members'. We hold stress in the same areas of our bodies and see similar health concerns. It is the way we hold our emotions that gets stored as memory and then is expressed through health.

Emotional memory in resonance is resonating with others at a similar frequency emotionally. We respond to emotional experiences similarly and connect with similar memories. Our life struggles seem to bear resemblance. We are in connection with others through our emotional memory as emotional resonance.

We connect with others with similar personalities. We share similar life experiences and emotional patterns of behavior. There is often a feeling of wonder how we could have met someone who we relate to so well. We may evolve and fall out of resonance with individuals and groups but with tendencies to move back into resonance. Can relationships be so random?

Emotional patterns are indicators of shared memory in resonance. We can see noticeable patterns of emotions as well as health concerns in family and other relationships. It is interesting to experience random encounters with others who have similar life struggles and health concerns. Could it be that we face similar emotional patterns in our lives?

Emotional resonance can be as encompassing as the universe. We may be in resonance with someone far across the globe and see similarities in form, personality, and mannerisms. Could these individuals experience similar life and health struggles? Could these individuals be part of groups in emotional resonance? We can learn a lot from those who are similar to us.

Our memory in resonance may be seen in a strong resemblance of another. We may see similar emotional patterns of behavior and interests. It is common to see similar features and personalities in those in similar fields of work. There is more reason to confirm this suggestion rather than deny it. Memory seems to be grouped in people who are in emotional resonance.

Our health is an expression of memory. Health imbalances can be seen as unresolved emotions in an area that has found resonance. We can see the fragmentation that has spanned across generations as similar health and life struggles. We are a reverberation of memory that has taken form. Balanced health is in our healing of fragmented emotional memory.

Emotional memory in resonance can be an outward indication of similarity. We can see how similar forms and emotional patterns of behavior may be indicators of similar health concerns. We may be part of shared groups of emotional memories. In our known resonance, we can heal together and express our memory as balanced health.

CHAPTER 3

Memory to Light

IT IS WELL KNOWN that light transfers information across space and time. It is a fixed law that keeps us bound to its specifics. Could it be that light carries information as memory across our being and through space and time? The nature of our being is intelligent beyond laws. We are infinite light beings connected to all memory as one light.

Scientists are in constant search for where our memories are stored. They are convinced that memory storage and retrieval are somewhere in neural circuits that form memory traces in our brains.[1] Could it be that our memories are not bound to the storage of our brains but imprint across all scales of our being and beyond? Opening our perception can expand research.

In a recent study, neuroscientist Susumu Tonegawa used a technique called optogenetics that modifies the genes of lab animals "so that their cells express a light-sensitive protein called channelrodopsin, derived from green algae."[2] Specific cells that were activated would glow during a learning event. Tonegawa said, "You can demonstrate those are the cells really holding the memory...because if you reactivate only those neurons with laser light, the animal behaves as if recalling memory."[3] It could instead be suggested that the cells that glow are transmitting or receiving messages, but there is nothing truly indicating that it is *stored* memory.

Could it be that our entire being uses light to encode memory? As a recent study found, "the optical properties of mitochondrial bundles in the retina may improve how efficiently the eye captures light."[4] The mitochondria may function as microscopic lenses helping to focus light. The senior author of the paper, Wei Li, stated, "Instead of being obstacles, the mitochondrial bundles seem to play a critical role in helping to funnel as much light as possible to the photoreceptors with minimal loss."[5] If mitochondria function to help focus light in the eyes, it could be suggested that mitochondria are used to help focus light as memory into the brain and across *all* cells of a biological being.

The intelligence of our being creates and imprints memories in a flash. It could be suggested that our memories are formed at their emotional frequency and imprinted in light as storage. Our memories, as information transferred by light, would reverberate across all our being and through space and time as their resonant frequency. We would then connect with memories of the past when we return to its resonant frequency. It is in our awareness of light that we can transform our emotional memories to resonate with balance.

Every emotion is imprinted at its frequency as memory. We are the frequency that we are feeling, and we express ourselves as that frequency, whether as an emotional expression or as our physical form. Our emotions are constantly being imprinted into the memory of our being and throughout the universe. Held fragmented resonant memories affect our health and influence the entire collective memory. We are all one light.

We are intelligent beings who imprint memory in light. Our memories show that they go beyond limitations. We recall memories without effort and our bodies express memory through old injuries. Our memories are not only visuals of the past but are expressed in our health. If memory imprints in light across our being, then it could be suggested that *we are light*.

Emotional Frequency and Light

What is it that truly activates memories? We recall memories in a flash without any effort. Scientists modify genes to see neuronal circuits light up and believe they hold memory. What is it that signals light to carry information to recall or store memory? Could it be the emotional frequency of our being that sends the message to light?

We are emotional beings. Our emotions hold frequencies that affect our entire being. We can all feel the difference between being in peace and feeling anger. Our current emotions seem to activate similar emotional memories. It could be suggested that our emotional frequency of a moment triggers light to activate the memories that we remember.

Scientists continue to believe that our memories are stored in our brains. Animals are genetically modified to allow cells in the brain to light up when stimulated with hope to reveal memory. It would be interesting to study if using different frequencies stimulates a different neural response, instead of continuing to think that lit cells *contain* stored memory.

Memories can appear in an instant. We often wonder what could have made us think of a particular memory, while other times the experience we are in reminds us of a past event. Our emotions are expressed as the frequency that we are in a moment. It again sounds plausible that the frequency of our emotions signals light to carry information for memory recall.

Is frequency the answer to learning more about memory? We can heal unresolved pain if we begin to see the connection between our current emotional frequency and memories. We often stay attached to our emotional pain and justify our reasoning. We *become* the frequency of a past event. It is our frequency that activates our memories, which can then affect our health.

Everyone has a personal frequency of his or her being. Our entire being resonates at a specific frequency that is unique to us. Different areas of our bodies will take on a frequency that is of balance or imbalance and it is vital to our being to balance our emotions and health. We are beings of light and it is in our balance that we shine.

The frequency of our being connects us with our past memories. Our current emotional frequency and the memory of our being are the signals for light to recall memory. Memories that come in a flash represent the frequency of our being as a sharp similarity to past memory. Our memories are recalled as the frequency at which they were transferred via light to memory.

We are intelligent beings. We use our senses even when unaware. Even the subtlest of feelings triggers a wave of information. Our being recalls the different frequencies from our past and connects us with memories that align with those feelings. It is in our awareness that we respond to our feelings with balance and calm. We express the frequency that we are.

Memories can be seen as being activated by emotional frequency and carried by light. Our emotions are indicators of our frequency. We can learn by the response that we have to the memories that appear. Scientists can learn from using different frequencies in memory studies. We can go beyond the brain as the holder of memory and appreciate that we are beings of light.

Light in Form

Our form represents the personal frequency and memory of our being. We are the memory of all previous experiences, existing as form. We live only as the frequency of our form to navigate through our lives to balance the memory of our being. We suffer in our ignorance as being only our bodies. In our awareness, we live as part of the whole as light in form.

Our true nature is made up of light waves with different particles and waves. Our soul is the memory of all our previous experiences, including past lives. Memory manifests as form based on the resonance of our being. We unify with family memory to help us realize our life goals. We are memory as light in form as a biological being.

In fact, Dr. Fritz-Albert Popp, the German scientist who coined the term *biophoton* and was the inventor of biophoton theory, notably stated, "We know today that man, essentially, is a being of light."[6] He explained that biophotons originate from a coherent photon field within the living organism.[7] His work shows that DNA in a living cell stores and releases photons, creating biophotonic emissions that may hold the key to illness and health.[8]

As light beings who have taken on form, we have the innate ability to heal through frequency. We are frequency that communicates messages of balance or imbalance. To heal, our minds must unite with our true nature as light. It is in the acknowledgment of the light that we are that we can truly heal.

We are memory-encoded light in form. It is the memory of our being that is the source of the form that we are. We take on similar features as others in resonance and are positioned to have similar life experiences. We resonate with the memory of others who are trying to accomplish similar goals. As our form we can experience life and heal memory.

We are born from memory but soon forget our truth. In our forms, we live our individual lives, but we are illuminated from one light. We exist as all previous memory of our being and live to balance our memory. We suffer in not knowing the true nature of our being as we attach to emotional experiences in hope for security. In our remembrance of truth, we live in peace.

In the peace of our being, we live in the awareness of our collective unity. We see where we individually need healing to come together to heal collectively. We can see the memory of our being through our emotions and life experiences. It becomes clear that our emotions affect the collective. It is in this depth of knowing that we heal to live together as one light.

As light in form, we are powerful beyond the conditioned narrative we are led to believe. Each and every one of us is light in form who has the power to heal our health and lives. We do not need excessive medical interventions, poisons under the guise of medicine, or government assistance. We have the innate ability to heal. We are light.

In our light as form, we shine as the memory of our being. Our resonant frequency holds all previous experiences as memory, and we are an expression of it. Light is merged with the particles of our form to make one entity. Our true nature is light, and we share this light with the entire universe as one light.

One Light

The universe is a creation illuminated by light. Patterns of memory radiate as light waves in all their creativity. We see and feel expressions of frequency all around us that reverberate through the collective. We are illuminated to shine as our own light while also sharing the light of the universe as one light.

All existence is light vibrating in its uniqueness. We live as individuals through our personal light and memory while still being connected to all light and memory. It is as our personal expression of frequency that we share ourselves in constant communication with the whole. We are individual expressions of light connected as one light.

As one light, patterns of geometry unfold in all their beauty and radiate through its light. Fields of resonance hold similar patterns in unity to evolve with greater intricacy, sending information from light to memory. Patterns of memory shine through creation as beauty in all its forms. The universe expresses all its creativity as it shines as its expression of light.

In our personal light, our frequency reverberates into the collective. Our emotions, actions, and behaviors are shared throughout the universe. To know the truth of light and memory is to know the emotional impact we have on the health of the collective. It is a great responsibility to know. Healing our personal light is healing for all as one unified light.

We are a part of a vast collective expression of light. We see expressions of frequency in all creative forms and feel vibrations of frequency when close to or in the absence of visible forms. As the light beings that we are, we are affected by the energy all around us, and our energy affects others. To see ourselves as one with all light brings us closer to healing us all.

To be unaware of our true nature as light keeps us in separation. We cannot heal personally or as a collective if we stay bound to the limitations of being one mind and body. To be divided in thought is to live divided in darkness. To be open to the light that we are is to heal the light of our being and extend healing into the collective.

In the intelligence of light, we are not bound to dimensions. We resonate with fields of frequency that go beyond our conceptual minds. We emotionally resonate with others on similar paths as ours. It is in the emotional frequency of our being that we input balance or imbalance into the field of the collective. Our individual balance is unlimited healing for all as one light.

To heal our memory is to heal our unresolved emotional pain. Our emotions impact our health and our health further impacts our emotions. The emotional frequency of our being affects all areas of our lives and is imprinted into the collective memory. We are light in form and it is in the awareness of our light that we heal to express the light that we are.

As one light, we share a universal creation of memory and frequency. We are light beings born of memory and connected as one light. Our fragmented emotional memories impede us from living as one light. We can heal the emotional frequency of our being and transfer healing memory to come together as one resonant light in peace.

CHAPTER 4

Memory and Behavior

IF WE ARE ALL one, how can there be so much division between us? How can we think bad thoughts and hate others? We live through painful memories that have us acting out in ways that go against our truth. We distract ourselves from remembering our true nature. Our behavior becomes part of the collective memory. It is in our awareness that we share peace, not pain.

The most pressing question of all time is, "How can there be a higher power that allows bad actors to cause suffering in our world?" We are quick to find blame without seeing that we all contribute to our shared being. We have forgotten our true nature as being one with all and we see through a lens of separation. Remembering our truth holds all answers.

Our pain has us going against the true nature of our being. We live so close to our pain that we cannot see our truth. We behave in ways that have us aiding our ego-self without knowing who we truly are. We see only through our conditioned perception as separate beings divided against each other. Our believed division has become visible through our behavior.

The memory of our being moves toward balance through our behavior. We can see good behavior as being consistent with truth while seeing poor behavior as being far removed from the truth of who we are. We feel separate in our suffering and it shows in how we treat others and ourselves. Struggles in our lives are indicators that we are out of balance with truth.

We distract ourselves from remembering our truth. We use clever ways to numb our pain, without realizing that there is such a thin veil between our suffering and our true nature. We complicate life by getting caught in thinking that we are only our body and mind. Our freedom is already within us; we just have to be open to it.

We close ourselves down in our perceived separateness. We attach to thoughts of hate and division and move further away from others, which is to move further away from ourselves. Society is slipping into more confusion with conditioning and is getting lost in division. We must see that we are all one and come into balance and peace.

Our behavior is shared with the collective. The contents of our individual minds are shared with all. Our thoughts of division and discord become part of the collective memory and we stay stuck in cycles of perpetual conflict. Collective peace begins with the healing of our individual memory to come together in harmony as one shared light.

It is our responsibility to be the peace that we are and contribute peace into our shared memory. Our poor behavior disrupts the balance of our true nature as love. It is through our peace that we act with love and compassion for all of life.

The recognition of our truth has us knowing in depth that our behavior matters for the balance of all to live in peace.

There is no division where there is love. We must stand strong in the face of hate and see truth as love. To know our true nature is to know that we are not our painful memories. We can live as the peace that we are and shine our light through our behavior as peace. In living as the love that we are, we stand true to the true nature of our being as peace.

Living Painful Memories

All our memories live through us, but it is our painful memories that come through our life struggles. We see struggles in our health, relationships, and work areas of our lives. We see our personal, ancestral, and collective traumas live through our experiences. We choose familiar lifestyle patterns and live in conflict. To heal our painful memories is to live free.

Our memories are held as patterns of balance or imbalance and show through our life experiences. Patterns appear, and if we are aware, we can see all our past experiences get worked out in our everyday lives. We can prevent living through feelings of pain by giving attention to our behaviors. It is in our behavior that we see unresolved pain.

Our painful memories are clearly seen in our life struggles and behaviors. Our struggles in our health, relationships, and work lives can all be traced back to our unresolved pain. Our struggles are indicators of a conflict within. The memory of our being is *always* trying to balance out through experience. We just need to not fight the flow of life.

We choose familiarity over change. We get involved in the same types of relationships that align with past traumatic frequency. We work jobs that go against our values, live in places where we are not happy, and dream of retirement for freedom. We live in conflict and against our truth. Freedom is to live in our truth.

To live in our past traumatic pain only brings more pain. We bring our pain into relationships that will inevitably end. We cause ourselves more suffering and it further affects our health. In fact, "across several epidemiological studies, being or becoming divorced (or separated) is associated with increased risk for poor physical health and divorced men and women are more likely to die earlier from a range of different diseases." Researchers "found that up to two years after the end of a marriage, divorced adults who continue to emotionally struggle with their separation evidenced significantly higher [health concerns indicating] compromised immune functioning." Behaviors linked to the health of recently separated or divorced adults included drinking more, sleeping less, and engaging in less exercise.[1]

In our avoidance, our painful memories affect our health. Our unawareness has us adding on more pain to past traumas. We unseeingly walk into trouble through our lives as we live through childhood, ancestral, and other past traumas. It is in our awareness that we see memories trying to balance out. In our balance, we can live a life of freedom.

Living free without suffering means healing our painful memories. Suffering is in our emotional attachments and our peace is living free of attachments. Our memories will always be there, but it is our frequency that changes with our awareness. Peace is knowing that we are light beings, and it is in this awareness that we live free.

Living through painful memories is seeing through a limited self. Our pain is very real, but it is in seeing through our limitation as being only one body and mind that we get caught in suffering. We become our pain. In the healing of our painful memories, we face our pain and end our emotional attachments. Our memories still live through us, but in our awareness, we live in peace.

Emotional Distractions

We see unresolved memory in our distractions. We find clever ways to distract ourselves from our emotional pain. We crave feeling a past frequency to feel safe in familiarity. Memory sparks a stimulus and we respond with distraction. Our habitual distractions become addictions. In our unawareness, we live distracted from truth.

Our distractions are emotional pain in disguise. We are most often unaware that we are distracting ourselves until time passes. Our unresolved memory is resonant within us and we feel it even when we are unaware. It is in our awareness that we catch our distractions and see the deeper reasons that underlie why we distract. Seeing the truth of our distractions brings our suffering to light.

Our behavior shows unresolved memory. We distract ourselves as we take on more work than we can handle. We eat, drink, do drugs, watch videos, play games, and scroll social media. We cleverly find something to do to distract ourselves from the feelings that can actually lead us to freedom. Our emotional distractions keep us in suffering.

Our distractions become part of our daily lives. Our repeated distractions become addictions; we become addicted to being distracted. We become dependent on something to distract us from our emotional pain as we move further away from our truth. Emotional distractions as addictions keep us in suffering. We *become* the addiction.

It is a common tactic in recovery programs to name our addictions. If someone is struggling with drinking alcohol, they say, "*I am* an alcoholic," "*I am* a recovering alcoholic," "*I am* in recovery," or "*I am* so many years sober." The person with the struggle becomes one with the label and is never able to see past the addiction.

In fact, according to the National Institute on Drug Abuse (NIDA), relapse rates for addictions show that 40 to 60 percent of people relapse after treatment.[2] The emotional memory is never addressed and healed completely. The person stays tethered to the addiction forever when they say "*I am* that." We are not labels; we are powerful beings of light able to heal our pain and live freely.

Our distractions keep us entangled with our unresolved emotional memory. We align with a past frequency as we become distracted. Familiarity feels safe, even when it is destructive. Every distraction keeps us from our truth. We stay in a loop of struggle.

Our distractions affect our health. We numb our emotional pain with food, caffeine, drugs, and alcohol—all of which are harmful to our health. We distract ourselves from the true nature of our being as we align with the memory that keeps us in our pain. To heal our health is to heal our emotions and live free of distraction.

Our distractions show us our unresolved memory. We can clearly see that where we distract is where we need healing. Our healing is in the depth of knowing that we are not our emotional pain and we are always safe as the true nature of our being. It is in our awareness that we stand in our truth and live undistracted.

Collective Behavior

Our collective behavior is an expression of our collective emotional memory. Collective traumas are seen in our personal behaviors, as well as in groups who share fields in resonance. Wars, pandemics, violence, and recessions bleed into the collective mind and influence our behaviors. It is in our personal behavior that we help to shift the collective.

We are all one collective memory but share fields of emotional resonance with others depending on our frequency. Our behaviors can resemble the behaviors of those we have never encountered or even been aware of. In our emotional resonance, we share a field of memory that has us engaging in similar behaviors. It is in our balanced frequency that we extend peace into the collective.

Traumas pervade the collective memory. We feel the collective pain and suffering while we can also see who we are in resonance with in our behavior. We align with the views of others and may act out in ways we never have before because our frequency was in emotional resonance with similar behaviors. It is in this knowing that we share peace to live in peace.

Collective behaviors affect the health of the collective. We live in a society where people follow the latest news narrative and live with fear and anxiety. Our collective health is at risk as long as people stay asleep and follow the agenda of the pharmaceutical companies, unhealthy food industries, and watch toxic news that directs us to these unhealthy ways of living.

We group together in our distractions. Our behavior feels justified when we are part of a group that engages in the same behaviors. Smoking, drinking coffee and alcohol, doing drugs, and engaging in social movements become a false backbone of a group. Habitual distractions are harder to shift once established in groups. We must be willing to stand independent of a group, undistracted.

Our collective memories are seen through our collective behavior. We see historical traumas living through the present. Emotional pain becomes a diagnosis, fears become violence, and the cycle repeats. We live in perpetual suffering as we become complacent with the chaos of the world. We must be willing to break the cycle of pain. The healing of one is healing for all.

Our personal behavior affects the collective. We contribute to collective suffering every time we shame ourselves, are unkind to others and ourselves, or act in immoral ways. It is in our personal healing that we help heal our shared memory. Our behavior affects the collective because we are one with the collective.

We are one conscious mind. Our behaviors, thoughts, and feelings extend into the collective memory. It is in our awareness that we share peace in unity and not pain in division. In our peace, we live life as one unified being. We feel our contribution truly matters to help lift the collective out of suffering. Our peace is peace for all.

We are an expression of the whole. The collective memory shows through our individual expression of behavior. It is in our pain that we see ourselves as individuals who are separate. We heal individually and collectively in the depth of knowing that we are all one light. In our healing, we share the light that we are through our connection as one collective memory of light.

CHAPTER 5

Emotional Regression

THE DAILY STRESSORS OF life begin to seep through our emotions. We break out of our emotional balance and regress to the frequency of imbalanced emotions. It is in the conflict between familiarity and the true nature of our being that we see life as difficult. We get caught in the cycle of struggle and forget what we know. Our past becomes the present.

Our past emotional traumas rise to the surface of our minds in moments of stress. We may have balanced our emotions only to regress emotionally when triggered. We overlook truth as we easily fall into the groove of familiarity. In a flash, we become our past emotions and traumas. We see before us the person we transformed into falling into struggle again.

Society as a whole is stressed. According to the American Psychological Association (APA), recent stress levels have been influenced by mass fear, rising inflation, and global uncertainty.[1] The APA further found that pandemic-related stress "was associated with unhealthy weight gain and increased drinking."[2] We have forgotten our innate peace and live with collective struggle.

Increased stress in our lives challenges our emotional balance. We align with our past emotional memories and fall back into old behaviors. We stay with what feels familiar and ignore what we know. In our avoidance, emotional pain and health concerns become the center of our attention. Life becomes difficult again.

Our imbalanced emotions affect our health, relationships, and work lives. We live in conflict with the true nature of our being and live in confusion. Poor decision-making becomes part of our daily lives as we forget our truth and look outside of ourselves for answers. It is in our emotional balance that we see and know truth within.

We regress emotionally in how we limit ourselves. We attach to one way of knowing and impede ourselves from flowing with life. We live for what is familiar and stay stuck in past ways of being that have not worked before. Our stress compounds as we go further into struggle. We think that life is working against us while unaware that we can free ourselves at any time.

Our emotional balance is in our awareness. We regress to the memories of experiences that made a strong impression on us and they are expressed with intensity. Our memories are shown through our emotions and switching from struggle to peace is in our power through awareness. We can stay in struggle or live in peace.

We live as the frequency of memories that we hold as emotional attachments. Our unresolved emotions are resonant within us as an imbalanced frequency. In the freedom from emotional attachments, we live in the flow of life.

Healing our emotional memories and balancing our frequency is to live in the present moment in peace.

To live aware and in the present is to be unshakable to daily challenges. We stay emotionally balanced and in alignment with the true nature of our being. We flow with life, no matter the circumstances. We exchange familiarity for living truth and stay true to the truth of our being. We remember our past to progress, not emotionally regress.

Daily Living

Compounding stress leading to overwhelm has complicated our lives. People chase ways to attain more pleasure, money, and power in this world. As pressures and demands increase, we move further away from the true nature of our being. We are easily shaken out of our calm and get annoyed by the behaviors of others. Stress becomes a part of our daily routine.

We live through repetition. We keep our days predictable to stay comfortable and safe in what we know. We add on more tasks that cleverly help us avoid what can bring us true peace. It is the added pressures that test our calm and have us regressing to old emotional behaviors. We get caught in the cycle of stress.

People feel more successful as they become busier. We constantly pursue a higher societal status. Having more money and power is seen as being in good standing with society, while those who struggle financially are seen as weak and failures. We lose sight of the truth of who we are and attach to false definitions of success.

Our conditioned minds override our true nature. We believe that our daily stressors are all that shape our existence. We try to distract ourselves from the chaos of life, but we get consumed by emotional stress. Life only gets louder, trying to get our attention to come back to the true nature of who we are. It is up to us to listen.

As stress builds, we get rattled out of our calm. We get bothered by the smallest of noises and are emotionally triggered by the most nonthreatening comments. The behaviors of others become especially annoying and we feel pushed to the end of our ability to cope. It is in our awareness that we stay emotionally balanced and in peace.

In our unawareness, we regress emotionally. We get caught in our daily struggles and only see as far as the emotions involved. We stay stuck there until we realize that moments of stress show us where healing is needed. It is in our awareness that we see opportunity where we saw struggle and we bring balance to imbalance.

Our emotional balance helps us navigate circumstances that happen out of our control. Life will always present us with challenges and the way we handle them is within our power. Healing our unresolved emotional pain keeps us in a state of calm. It is hard to knock us down in challenging times when we stand in emotional balance.

Constant hard problems in our lives demand a closer look as to why they are happening. Are the people in our lives helping us rise, or are they holding us back? Do the jobs we hold light us up in the morning and help us feel that we are giving back and not just earning a paycheck? Are our relationships truly healthy, or are they toxic to our peace? Emotional balance should not be hard work.

In our emotional balance, our days become easier and we live in peace. We see false power as a hindrance to living a balanced life. We see added stressors as being against our true nature and choose to be true to ourselves. We stand strong in the face of challenges because our emotions are balanced. Peace is in our daily routine.

Conflict Within

We feel pulled in different directions. There is something within us that knows to go one way, but we go the other. We find ourselves living in conflict with our personal values in exchange for familiarity. Our lives become chaotic and we think the world is working against us, so we react. In our struggles, we close ourselves down to truth. We live with internal conflict.

Why do we put ourselves through struggle? Our lives in conflict feel so familiar that we go along with the struggle. We go against what we know will bring us peace because we think it is far out of reach. It is our lifelong conditioning that has us believing there is no way out of struggle. Our freedom is in the depth of knowing that we can free ourselves at any time.

To be in conflict within is to go against truth. In our conflict, we live against the true nature of our being, as well as our personal truth as values. We may follow a spiritual path but then live in conflict between knowing truth and living truth. We get so stuck in our familiar structures and emotional attachments that we stay with conflict.

In our conflict, we feel drawn in the direction of more conflict. We choose the familiar path that leads us right back to struggle. We think that there is something this time that will be different, but we are faced with the same story. It is as if we embrace the conflict in its familiarity. We sit confused, without knowing that the answers to our problems lie in the conflict.

Living in conflict within has us reacting to the difficulties of life. Our problems in life feel inescapable, so we live in constant response. We react with anger and seek pleasure to take the pain away. We ask ourselves, "Why does this always happen to me?" We react and blame our struggles on others, the world, or karma.

As light and memory that have taken form, we exist as a being of cause and effect. The universe does not know good or bad, but only balance and imbalance. It is we who label experiences because we adhere to the laws of society. We know within what good moral behavior is and is not. It is our action through awareness that results in a balanced effect.

To be in conflict within is to be in contradiction with truth. To live truth is to know that struggle is our response to living against truth. In our struggle, we live against the flow of life and expect life to flow. Balance in life is a result of living truth and we just need to remember truth to be free of conflict. It is in our conflict that we live disorderly lives.

Our lives are complicated. We take on more work, more stuff, and more stress. We become worried about societal success. We feel defined by the titles we hold and then we complain about stress. We have to ask what kind of life we want to live. If we aim to live a simple life, then life would take on a stress-free tone.

In our grounded awareness, we are settled in calm. We live open to truth and feel in alignment with life. We know what direction to go because we are living true to ourselves. It is in our calm that we respond to life with awareness. We flow with life to live in balance. We live in peace within.

Forgetting through Avoiding

Our emotional attachments are strong. We hold on so tightly to what feels familiar that we lose all previous knowledge that could help us avert pain. Our actions show that we are ignorant to truth, even though we have been through the same struggle before. How do we forget? Our hidden pain has us avoiding truth only to repeat painful experiences again. We cleverly forget through avoidance.

We may have opened to truth in the past only to shut it down to feel secure in our emotions. In our false security, we distance ourselves from the knowing of our true nature. We fit ourselves back into the struggle of life in exchange for familiarity. Sadly, we may even be aware of our actions, but do them anyway. We use avoidance to forget.

In our avoidance, the conflict that we hold within leads to more stress. In fact, a ten-year avoidance coping study found that participants exhibited more chronic and acute stressors over the assessment period that resulted in depressive symptoms.[3] We may think that we are averting pain through avoiding, but we are creating more struggles.

In our struggles, there are emotional attachments. The feeling of losing something that we are emotionally attached to brings us fear. The unsettling feeling has us forgetting what we know as we cling to the familiar. We avoid what can bring us peace and we rationalize our position. If we are justifying being in struggle, then it would be wise to reevaluate our view.

We often look back over the years and regret our past actions. We think, "If I only knew then what I know now." It is in our awareness that we can clearly see our present struggles as going against truth. We can see attempts to repeat experiences as a path leading us to pain. Our insight into truth lies within our memories. Our memories are there to guide us to peace.

Forgetting through avoidance suppresses the knowing of our true nature. We feel emotionally safe in our ignorance. We have been conditioned to believe that pain and struggle are the ways of life, so we live with them. Living within our ego-structures keeps us busy and focused on struggle. To face our pain is to be true to who we are and focus on the peace of our being.

We go against ourselves when we repeat painful experiences. We avoid truth in our attraction to the frequency of our pain and get caught in the chaos again. We sleepwalk through life only to watch many years go by with pain and suffering. In our avoidance, we hinder ourselves from progressing emotionally in life. We stay stuck.

Remembering averts avoidance. We realize truth through memory. The ignorance of our true nature and past experiences is illuminated with a depth of knowing. To forget keeps us in the struggle of life. We endlessly chase a solution to our problems, as if the answer is somewhere outside of us. To remember truth is to be without attachments and live free and in peace.

True freedom is powerful. It is in truth that we live free of avoidance and stay focused on truth. We are free of the attachments to outcomes and live in the flow of life. The healing of our emotions and the memory of our being has us settled in peace and calm. We emotionally progress as we remember our truth and live free.

CHAPTER 6

Emotional Impact

OUR ENERGY DROPS AS we experienced in the past. We know the feeling well. We have been living in the darkness of our pain and feel wedged between the trauma that we never healed and health patterns emerging once again. Our emotional pain takes hold of our mind and we begin to lose our ground. We become emotionally impacted.

We know all too well the feeling of being emotionally drained. We get attached to our emotional pain and cannot seem to shake it. Life feels difficult and unfair in our pain, so we withdraw. There is a feeling of safety in our familiar suffering, so we stay with it. It is in our suffering that we live in the dark.

We lose ourselves in the dark. We become our pain and suffer in our attachment. Our dark thoughts consume every part of our waking life as well as our dream state. We get caught in the loop of struggle with our suffering locked into the memory of our being. We feel stuck with no way out of our pain. We live impacted by past traumas and the suffering of the present.

According to the World Health Organization (WHO), in 2021 there were approximately 280 million people world-wide diagnosed with depression.[1] In 2022, they stated that the recent pandemic triggered a 25 percent increase in the prevalence of anxiety and depression worldwide.[2] All of our lives have been emotionally impacted in some way, no matter the data.

We are emotionally impacted by our emotional attachments. We become reactive when what we are attached to is threatened in any way. Fear grips us at the core of our being and we lose our ability to make sound decisions based on truth. We create more chaos in our lives and get caught in the frequency of our past traumas.

In our emotional suffering, we pick up our favored distractions and addictions. We feel magnetized to what can possibly numb our pain but learn that it only makes it worse with associated problems. Our past traumas come back to haunt us as we get trapped in the repetition of our life struggles. Our pain lives through us, even when we are distracted.

In our pain and struggles, we see familiar health symptoms emerge. We live in alignment with our past trauma frequency and accept it all as part of our struggle. We may recognize what is happening but only know how to stay with the pain. Our entire being is resonating at an imbalanced frequency and we feel stuck in the chaos.

We are emotionally impacted when we are stuck in any way. We are settled in calm when our emotions are balanced. We stand firm in the face of personal challenges and societal disorder. It is in our personal disorder that we live on the edge, as if waiting for the next problem to arise. Peace and freedom are always available to us—we just have to be open to them.

In our freedom, we feel alive and well. We are aware of our emotions and are open to living true to who we are without suffering. We see the imbalance in the repetition of our pain, and we free ourselves of the burden. In our clarity, we live grounded in truth and stand strong in moments of emotional challenges. We live free and in peace.

Health Regression

We have been living in the darkness of our pain and are now seeing the emotional impact on our health rise up again. We thought we were healed while disease was unknowingly developing. We have become our pain and can now see our health in regression.

Emotional memory shows through our symptoms. Health symptoms are a clear indicator that the frequency of our pain is still resonating as imbalanced. Our health in regression is more than statistical data showing duration of time for a disease recurrence. There are many factors, such as our diet, lifestyle, and emotional well-being, that influence our physical health.

The return of our health symptoms demands us to evaluate the true underlying cause. We go deep into the darkness of our minds to find clarity. In our clarity, we can see the impact that our unresolved emotions have on our health. Recurring health symptoms are guiding us to heal our emotions. To truly heal is to see our emotional pain as a hindrance to balanced health.

We think that we are healed until we get emotionally activated again. The same symptoms reappear, but with more force. New symptoms start to develop, and we wonder what is happening, as if they were occurring out of nowhere. We feel overwhelmed by our symptoms, so we book a doctor's appointment. It is worse than we thought—we get diagnosed with a disease.

In the frequency of pain, we see ourselves only as our body and mind. Our true nature is far from our thoughts. We get sucked into the medical system to fix, cure, and remove our health symptoms with the conditioned belief that we do not have the power to end our pain. In our pain, we suffer. We become our health symptoms. We become our emotional pain.

Health regression happens over time. Diseases develop long before symptoms arise. We do not just wake up one morning with a serious disease. It is in the assessment of our emotional pain that we can find a connection between our emotions and our health. Our imbalanced emotions affect the frequency of our being, and we get stuck in our pain and struggle.

Seeing the impact of our emotions in our health further impacts our emotions. Challenges in our health affect our daily lives. Our emotional challenges keep us in a continuous cycle of suffering. Balanced health needs balanced emotions. It is in our calm that we clearly see the threat that imbalanced emotions can have on our health.

To be in balanced health is to live proactively. Healing our pain requires our participation. Living in avoidance can lead to health imbalances that could be prevented. Past traumas can be difficult to face, but there is freedom on the other side of our pain. Balanced health is dependent on balanced emotional health and it is available to all of us.

Balanced health is in our power. In our emotional awareness, we live true to who we are and our balanced emotions shows through our health as balanced. We live actively in our healing without waiting for a devastating health event to arise. We live true to our being in balance and in our light.

Dimmed Light

We are emotionally impacted by many life experiences. We get hurt and energetically shut down an area of our being where we later see a health concern arise. The frequency of our unresolved emotional pain shows through our low energy. We live in the darkness of our pain and forget the light that we are. We live as a dimmed light.

We are beings of light. We feel filled with light and energy when we are healthy and strong. In our light, our personality shines with exuberance and there is a sparkle seen in our eyes. In the darkness of our pain, there is a noticeable dullness in our appearance. We lose the sparkle in our eyes and it is apparent that we have been emotionally impacted in some way.

In our pain, we can feel we will never experience happiness again. We become attached to how life should have unfolded, or what we do not have but wanted, and we lose the trueness of ourselves. We suffer in our emotional attachments and the happiness that is inherent within us is veiled through years of pain. We live in the dark.

In the darkness of pain, our health is impacted. In fact, Professor Fritz-Albert Popp conducted studies on cancer patients. "In every instance, these patients had lost...natural periodic rhythms as well as their coherence. The lines of internal communication were scrambled. They had lost their connection with the world. In effect, their light was going out."[3]

Our painful life experiences grip us at the core of our being. We get stuck in our pain and health symptoms start to show. We get caught in the cycle of medical interventions and our light dims lower. We become disempowered and move further away from the powerful beings that we are and live dependent on the tools of medicine.

Unawareness of the impact that our emotions have on our being is a danger to our health. The emotionally challenging times of our lives demand healing immediately to prevent health concerns from arising. To push emotional pain away is to invite more in. In our avoidance, we live in suffering as a dimmed light.

Living as a dimmed light is being in suffering. We cannot fake happiness. A facade cannot change the imbalanced frequency of our unresolved emotional pain. We can see it clearly in our life struggles and it is up to us to notice it and take action to heal. To fear healing is to be in constant opposition to the true light that we are. There is no fear in truth.

We live as our light in truth. Living true to the true nature of our being, as well as our values, dispels the darkness of suffering. In truth, confusion is exchanged for clarity. We see peace where there was pain. Life flows with no room for suffering. As a dimmed light, we stay attached to our pain. Our light is enveloped in darkness.

In our light, we hold no emotional attachments to life experiences. We live free of suffering in the depth of knowing that we are not the painful events of our lives. We flow through life without getting stuck in the darkness of pain. It is in our emotional balance that we live illuminated as the light beings that we are.

Becoming Our Pain

Everyone has some kind of pain that they hold. We are emotional beings, and some experiences make strong impressions. We become attached to our pain and it gets locked into our memory. Our health suffers through it, so we consult friends and go from doctor to doctor. Our unresolved pain turns into an endless search for emotional support. We become our pain.

Our emotional healing is foundational to all areas of our health. Our lives revolve around our emotional pain as we attach to our painful life stories. We speak in terms starting with "I" as we proclaim, "*I* have this disease" or "*I* had this experience or procedure." We continually speak our pain into existence without knowing that our freedom lies in nonattachment.

In our pain, we live in waiting. We wait for our health symptoms to disappear as we push truth aside. We submit to endless surgeries, thinking they are a cure and then live attached to statistics while waiting for a date to come and pass. We become one with our disease, along with the drugs and tools we need for assistance. We wait as we live through a disease name.

We become our pain when we feel better after having a named diagnosis. Linking a name to symptoms can somehow make everything feel better, like we have a hold of things. Yet it is a name that keeps us attached while we go from doctor to doctor to cure the named disease. Our health suffers as we attach to a false sense of security.

We lock our pain into memory in our search for emotional support. We talk about it with friends, passing acquaintances, and endless doctors of many disciplines. We attach to an outcome and live in hope of feeling better about ourselves. Our emotional pain holds its place of imbalanced frequency. We live in perpetual suffering.

Our emotional experiences make a strong impact on our mind. We become fixated on our story and it takes over our lives. We engage in activities and conversations that keep us attached to it. We search for answers outside of ourselves and find frustration and pain. True answers are always available to us. Truth is at the depth of our knowing.

Our unresolved emotional pain keeps us tied to suffering. To live in avoidance of healing keeps us in a continuous cycle of pain. We say we are fine, but then we recite a list of life experiences and health concerns that name our pain. We see our unresolved pain in our everyday lives as we live through the frequency of our imbalanced emotions.

We go through repeated experiences to get our attention. In our unawareness, we suffer. We become our experiences as we forget our true nature. We take action in areas that keep us in suffering and see inaction where we would see truth. If we are in pain, we are not living as the truth of who we are. We are living emotionally attached to pain.

We are light beings; we are not only our body and mind. We are indeed emotional beings and our health can be impacted by our emotions. Our healing lies in the depth of knowing that we are pure conscious awareness. To live as one with our pain is to give up freedom. We have the innate power to heal our emotions and live in peace.

PART II

How Our Health Impacts Our Emotions

CHAPTER 7

Health Memory

THE HEALTH MEMORY OF our being remembers what we try to forget. It responds in the same way as the previous times it was activated. It is in these responses that we see attempts for balance. Our avoidance, as well as our interventions, prolongs our suffering. We stay tied to the frequency of imbalance as our health experiences are locked into memory.

All health concerns lead back to balancing the memory of our being. The impact of our emotions activates our health memory and we see the effects. It is we who complicate health matters with forceful interventions that further delay true healing. Our healing is in balancing our emotions to balance our memory. Our balanced health is in our power.

Our imbalanced frequency shows through our health. Our unresolved memory has us reaching for the same foods, beverages, substances, or activities that previously affected our health. We think we can get passed our health being affected, but memory always comes through to create balance.

We unknowingly live in resonance with imbalanced health memory. We ignore signs that can prevent further health symptoms. We accept disease diagnoses and fight back with medical interventions. Life revolves around our health concerns, even though we may brush them off as not a problem. We live attached to fragmented frequency until we heal our unresolved memory.

The memory of our being continues to fragment in our imbalance. We walk around in a fog and struggle to make clear decisions. We repeat unhealthy lifestyle habits as a daily routine. Our bodies and minds become toxic in our unawareness. We spiral down into feeling trapped in our struggles. It is in our health struggles that we have tipped the scales way out of balance.

In our attempts for balance, we lose our connection with truth. We see memory come through as it did before and, instead of seeing it for its attempt for balance, we anxiously look for outside assistance. We live bound to external causes of health concerns as we strengthen the imbalance of our being. We chase hollow solutions and move further away from truth.

The memory of our being cannot be avoided. In our effort to escape pain, we end up suffering more. There is an extra nudge to get our attention with each progression of health symptoms. We may be told that our health concerns are age-related or linked to previous diagnoses, but memory comes through for balance. Our healing is in facing our pain in order to become free.

Limitations to our way of life grip us at the core of our being. All our focus goes to our current health concerns and we become one with it. We further affect our emotions by feeling limited without realizing that limitations are in our emotional attachments. It is in our depth of knowing that we are not our body and mind alone; we are pure conscious awareness as a witness.

The health memory of our being reminds us to remember truth. Our health is a significant indicator of balance or imbalance. It is in our awareness that we see the memory that is cleverly being shown through our health concerns. Avoidance will only prolong our suffering and make it worse through time. It is through our health memory that we unlock true health and freedom.

Resonant Health

We often notice imbalance in our health more than balance. Being sick, or getting diagnosed with a disease, weighs on us emotionally. We resonate with familiarity and get stuck in our limitations and struggles. Our health is in alignment with the memory of our being and we know our health status when we inquire within. The knowing of our resonant health can help lead us to balance.

The strength of our health can quickly be assessed in our awareness. We know deep within if we are in balance or not and what needs to be done. Our resonant health is the health that we align with and need to be aware of to come into balance. Avoidance, carelessness, or tolerance can turn into major health concerns. In our awareness, we see the needed balance.

Health symptoms are there to help us. Symptoms are indicators of what needs our attention. A shift in thinking from seeing our symptoms as limitations to knowing that the frequency of our being is trying to come into balance can help us heal. Life is constantly sending us messages for healing. Our physical health is a constant guide for our overall health.

Balancing our resonant health can begin with building a healthy immune system. The strength of our immune system determines how our body will respond to coming changes in our environment. Our diet is a main contributor to our health balance. Consuming sugar, fast and fake foods, and toxic chemicals will adversely affect the health of our being.

Antoine Béchamp, a rival to the inventor of germ theory, Louis Pasteur, foresaw the importance of the immune system to balance health. Béchamp argued that health was dependent on the host. He believed that a weakened and unhealthy terrain caused an individual to become vulnerable to disease.[1] Our imbalances invite disease in.

Imbalances in the memory of our being result from many lifetimes. We choose a path that will help awaken us to truth, but we fight it. Our resistance affects our health and then we suffer more emotionally. All experiences lead to balancing our memory. It is in our openness to the flow of life that we can align with balance, not pain.

The health we align with is usually based on familiarity. We resonate with the memory that can help us to heal our unresolved emotional pain. Sadly, we can endure some painful experiences through our health to balance our memory. It is through our emotional healing and a deep knowing within that we come into balance. Our healing leads us to freedom.

In our emotional pain, we get stuck in our limitations and struggles. We suffer with our health concerns, which further affect our health. Our emotional pain keeps us tied to health imbalances. It is our emotional attachments that keep us in suffering. Through nonattachment we feel inner peace, no matter the intensity of the experience.

The memory of our being reverberates messages through our health for our healing. We begin to heal when we live aware of our resonant health and align with balance. Our inquiry into our health shines light on where balance is needed. Our healing starts with a deep knowing that we can heal and live with balanced resonant health.

Health Impact

Our health is invaluable. Our body is the vehicle that carries us through life, so any restrictions affect us emotionally. In our health struggles, we turn toward our suffering and move further away from our true nature. We get caught in the loop of our emotions impacting our health and our health further impacting our emotions. We live emotionally attached to our pain.

Our health concerns have us laser-focused on them. Balanced health is the most valuable aspiration to have because without it, we feel limited. We get upset when we cannot eat a certain food or physically engage in an activity that we enjoy. Life becomes meaningless in our felt limitations. We live as one with our health concerns. We live in emotional pain.

Our unresolved memories give rise to our emotional attachments. We live in the frequency of our pain and attach to what feels familiar. Our health concerns are signs that show us our unresolved emotional memory. Seeing our health concerns as memory that needs to be balanced frees us from emotional attachments to our health limitations and pain.

In our health struggles, we focus our attention on the body and consider it damaged. We seek help from outside sources and are given limited options. We feel we must do as we are told, or consequences can be dire. In our fear, we submit to modern medicine and live attached to fixing ourselves as a malfunctioning body. We live powerless and detached from our true nature.

As health impacts our emotions, we become reactionary. We lose our calm and get angry about our health concerns. We feel unhappy in our struggle and take our emotions out on our relationships. Life becomes filled with stress as we live through the pain of our health. It is in the knowing of our true nature that we live grounded in calm.

Our health concerns take hold of our mind, and we succumb to thoughts of awful outcomes. We see everything in life as related to our health and then get entangled in destructive thinking. Our minds can take us down a dark path if we put our awareness aside. In our awareness, our thoughts are emotionally balanced.

In our health struggles, we embrace our suffering. We live bound to our conditioned beliefs about the meaning of health and diseases and live as though diseases through life are inevitable. We adhere to age-related tests with fear and accept declining health without question. The true meaning of health is in the knowing of the power of our true nature.

Our health impacts every area of our lives. True health is in the balancing of every part of our being. We use the knowledge about how our emotions impact our health and our health further impacts our emotions to heal and balance the memory of our being. It is with this knowledge that we can live free of health and emotional impacts in our lives.

In our balanced health, we live emotionally calm. We heal our emotions to balance our health to not further affect our emotions. We respect our body as a vessel and turn toward our true nature to live free of suffering. We live in the truth of our being and free of impacts to our health. We live healthy and in peace.

Health Initiative

Why are we such a sick society? Are all our health concerns inevitable parts of our lives or can they be prevented? We seem to be losing control of our health freedom. Agendas are getting stronger and people are following. We can be a healthier society if everyone stands in their own power and takes the initiative to heal individually. It is our health, our power.

There is always an excuse as to why taking care of our health needs to be pushed aside. Our lives have become busier. There are more responsibilities at work and home and fast food seems to fit into the schedules of many. We put our activities that distract us from our truth as first priority. To heal, we need to make our health our number one priority.

Health difficulties are not inevitable. Healing starts before a diagnosis. We have the power to live in balanced health, but we need to take the initiative. It is critical to see through the agendas that are being pushed for greed. Our balanced health is dependent on our awareness as our society gets trapped in the mainstream narrative. We are a sick and drugged society.

The United States and New Zealand are the only two countries that allow direct-to-consumer (DTC) advertising of prescription medications. In the US, DTC advertising increased from $2.1 billion in 1997 to $9.6 billion in 2016.[2] Harvard Medical School writes that "the main purpose of DTC drug advertising is to sell a product, not educate consumers."[3]

Our health is at risk when we listen to or read any mainstream news. We see sugar getting pushed in commercials and ads popping up in news articles. "The global industrial sugar market size was $37.62 billion in 2021. The market is projected to grow from $38.58 billion in 2022 to $46.56 billion by 2029."[4] The total consumer spending in the fast food industry in the US was $304.8 billion in 2021, while obesity prevalence was at 41.9 percent from 2017 to 2020.[5]

In addition to obesity, the CDC shows a total of 37.3 million people in the US to have diabetes (11.3 percent of the population). A total of ninety-six million people aged eighteen or older have prediabetes (38 percent of the adult population), while 26.4 million people aged sixty-five and older (48.8 percent) have prediabetes.[6] We are losing our health to marketing.

Our health freedom is at risk of being in the control of the government. We as a society are submitting to agendas that are taking away our right to be free. We must stand up for our rights, or we will lose them. We can vote with our dollars and not purchase the non-food items that are damaging our health. We can heal and not succumb to dangerous prescription drugs and surgeries that mutilate our people. We can live healthy and free.

A health initiative demands awareness to stand true to ourselves and to what we know is true. Our health cannot wait for willpower as a motivating factor. It withers away with the first emotional distraction. Our health needs the truth that we know at the deep core of our being so we can truly heal.

We can be a healthy society if we all initiate healing our personal health. We can live in control of our emotions and our health and prevent being impacted by subsequent emotional and health struggles. Our health memory balances out, and we see our resonant health stronger in our power. Balanced health is powerful and can lead us to freedom.

CHAPTER 8

Mental Health and Memory

W E ARE A LABELED and drugged society. We live scattered in thought to distract us from truth. We suffer from deep emotional traumas and many shut down in emotional pain. Our memories can haunt us for our entire lifetime as we live through our past emotional experiences. We live in separation with pain from the memories that run through our mind.

Our painful memories can take hold of our being and paralyze us. Our traumas leave deep grooves in our minds that we easily fall into, over and over. Our mental health is a result of our overall health but seems to take precedence because we let our thoughts run wild. It is in the chattering of our mind that we lose our ground.

In our pain, we search for relief and get labeled and drugged. Surveys conducted by the APA say, "We are facing a national mental health crisis that could yield serious health and social consequences for years to come."[1] In 2020, the total number of people taking psychiatric drugs in the United States was almost seventy-seven million.[2]

Medication will not heal the emotional memory of our experiences or our being. We live with both the memory of our being and the memory of our mind from our lifetime of experiences. Our memories from our experiences become part of the eternal memory of our being. Our mental health is dependent on healing our memory through emotional transformation.

Our scattered thoughts keep us distracted from our truth. We live fixed on our thoughts that keep us entangled in our daily troubles. Our minds need clarity for balance, but we rely on our chattering minds for answers. We use our words through our conditioned perception and stay mired in our troubled thoughts. Healing comes out of silence.

We heal when we face our pain. We shut down when we feel overwhelmed in our struggles. Life becomes very dark and lonely in our suffering. We feel separate from the world; our painful stories stay painful. We live through our past as our mind repeats our painful memories. It is in a deep knowing that we are not our pain that we can heal.

We stay attached to memories that we align in frequency. To see past our pain is to end our emotional attachments and introduce new ways of being. It is to change our frequency so we do not align with pain but with truth. It is in our suffering that we are far from the truth of who we are. We live as one with our thoughts and experiences, not as the truth of who we are.

Our thoughts are one with the entire universe. We are one collective conscious mind operating as individual bodies, minds, and emotions. In our struggles, we can draw on the knowledge of the universe for help. In this wisdom, we feel a deep knowing and belonging. It brings clarity and a feeling of support that cannot be explained.

In our balanced mental health, we live free of suffering. We live with clarity of mind and are focused on truth. Our lives become an expression of contentment as we align with memories of peace, not pain. We live mentally balanced and in the present. We know in depth that we are not the painful memories that run through our mind. We know our true nature is peace.

Deep Grooves of Trauma

Our traumatic memories come rushing into our minds with force. Our reaction is to succumb to the pain, so we avoid, numb, and react with strong emotions. We become fixed on our past while thinking that there is no way out. We suffer. The deep grooves of trauma get deeper with time as we live true to our minds and not to our true awareness.

Emotional trauma floods our minds with thoughts of pain. Our minds stay halted in time because we are focused on what happened in the past. We close ourselves down to the light beings that we are and live in darkness. Our thoughts of pain go against the true nature of our being as we live through a perception of time.

We can endure many painful experiences through a lifetime. Our brains adapt and change their structure and function in response to our experiences. Our repetitive behaviors and emotions reinforce the unhealthy ways our brains have learned to utilize maladaptive neural pathways.[3] It is because of our knowledge and reactions to our memories that our brains form new healthy connections.

Our mental health can be seen in many different external

behaviors. We can see our internal health in our surroundings. We see it in the friends we choose, family, work lives, and the way we live. Life is always showing us synchronicities and confirmations. In our awareness, we are able to see imbalances and live in balance.

Our reaction to our pain is very significant. We see expressed in emotions what we are holding in our minds. We live in attachment to our pain and watch it play out in our lives. Our avoidance, numbing, and strong emotions dig deeper grooves that become harder to change. We can heal our health and memory with new behavior. We can live in the peace of our true nature.

To live in suffering is to live true to our minds. Our thoughts of pain fill our minds and leave no room for clarity. We think that we are our painful experiences as we speak our pain into existence. We tell our stories to all who will listen. We suffer with the thoughts we believe to hold our true existence. It is in this belief that we suffer.

Our traumatic feelings and memories are very real. It is the pain that we hold in response to our experiences that separates us from our true nature. In our alignment with the deep knowing of truth, we live in peace. We flow with life in all its complexity. In our truth, we may remember our pain, but it is our reaction that changes. We express peace.

The deep grooves of trauma get deeper in an unchanging mind. Our thoughts remain on repeat without seeing any improvement for healing. Our mental health declines when we live fixed on our past. We live in deep suffering in our unawareness. Knowing our true nature has us focusing on truth. It is in our truth that we change our mind about our pain.

In our truth, our memories come in and flow out of our minds. We remain calm and composed knowing that we are not our painful experiences. We live in the flow of life while our thoughts are on truth, not pain. The deep grooves of trauma heal over time as we live true to the light beings that we are—not our minds.

Separate in Pain

In our search for truth in life, we are faced with hard challenges. In our struggles, we live in depression, frustration, and anger and feel a sense of separation. There is a clear division between our true nature and desires, but we close ourselves off from this knowing. Our being calls out to us to align with truth for peace, but instead we feel separate in pain.

We want the world around us to be the way we want in order to secure our peace and happiness. We try to control outcomes to satisfy our desires. We attach to people, places, things, events, and beliefs to fill a perceived gap of separation. It is in our attachments that our minds find easy ways to ignite emotions. The depth of our emotional attachments will determine our level of pain.

Our sensory systems can only take in so much before the need for a reset. To ignore the longing for truth is to live in a false sense of security. It is to live true to our desires and continue to live as separate beings. We push ourselves to the edge of collapse and ignore our true needs. Life becomes a cycle of struggle as we set ourselves up for a shut down.

Life indeed presents us with difficult challenges. We think that the universe is working against us when our desired plans do not go our way. Our response is to feel separate and cut off, without knowing that our feelings of separation lie in our perception. We are always one with all and not alone in our challenges. It is a knowing deep within that we cannot deny.

Our memory knows coherence as balance and fragmentation as imbalance. We feel in unity with all life in our natural state. Separation is a fallacy to our true reality. We live separate only from the falsity of our conditioned minds. It is in our balanced minds that we can think, speak, and act through the truth of balanced memory.

Our feelings of separation affect our health, which affects our emotions. To live in resistance to truth puts the memory of our being in a state of flux. Our thoughts in alignment with truth support the true peace of our being. We see it in our balanced health. In our perceived separation, we live against truth. We live imbalanced lives.

The memory of our being is always working toward balance. The state of our mental health is a reflection of our balance of memory. We feel separate in our imbalance. It is vital that we heal the memory of our being and align with truth for peace. We heal in life through adapting and changing. Our balanced mental health is in knowing that we are naturally peace, not pain.

Living as separate beings in pain affects the entire collective. We are one conscious mind living as individual beings and minds. Our experiences are one with the collective, not separate in isolation. We heal knowing that we are all in this experience together. The healing and peace of one mind is healing for the collective mind.

To know that we are together as one brings our search for truth to a new kind of end. Our challenges in life take on a different tone as we live with a deep sense of belonging and feel in peace. We live open to living in unity between truth and our existence. We hear the deep call from within to align with truth for peace and we unite to live open and free.

Lost Memories

Are lost memories retrievable? Can we erase memories that we find too painful? We shut out emotional pain in our struggle to cope. We think we can outwit pain, but our memories lie in the frequency in which they were created. Are we willing to go beyond conventional science to truly heal? Are we willing to face what we uncover? Memories are never lost forever.

We perceive memories as lost when we cannot remember them. We try to shut out memories that we prefer to lose. Our memories can be retrieved at a similar frequency that we were in at the time of past experiences. In our peace, all memories are available. It is our response to our memories that changes.

Scientists search for ways to erase memories in hope to develop more drugs for "mental disorders." They can activate cells to erase or evoke specific memories in rodent models and even implant false memories.[4] The erasure of neurons in the brain will only prolong our suffering as our being continues to feel. Our unseen memories will find a way to be seen again.

The brain is always adapting to its environment. We strengthen the neural pathways that are continuously being stimulated with similar information. Other pathways become weakened in the absence of use.[5] Our lost memories, whether avoided or shut out, are only obscured from view. To heal is to see that we access or block memories at the frequency that we are.

Can memories in Alzheimer's patients be recovered? Researchers found a link between depression and Alzheimer's disease in its preclinical stage, showing symptoms with brain amyloid.[6] This research to treat depression, however, does not include the alarming aluminum toxicity found in the brains of *all* Alzheimer's patients.[7] All factors need consideration.

In our struggle to cope with emotional experiences, we may either attach to the associated memories or avoid them. Either way, we form an attachment and remain tied to the frequency of the memories, even if we cannot remember them. They stay with us in their raw state until we transform our emotions and know in depth that peace is the nature of our being.

Our being is always aware of our memories. In our awareness, we can see our memories come through our actions. The specifics and visuals of past memories demand emotional balance. Our being is intelligent and knows when to shut out or reveal memories. In our emotional balance, we can face what we uncover. Facing our pain will set us free.

There is so much wisdom to uncover in life. Our lost memories are a key to our freedom. Our healing is in the depth of knowing that we can never truly lose our memories. It is in this alignment that we have a breakthrough. All we need to know comes through for our understanding. It is then that we remember truth in depth.

In our truth, we remember that our memories are always with us. They may be absent from view but lie in waiting in our balanced frequency. To know truth at the depth of our being opens us to the knowing that we have the power to heal without invasive scientific or medical interventions. To truly heal our mental health is to heal the memory of our being.

CHAPTER 9

Nutrition and Memory

WE TAKE IN NUTRIENTS through food and drink to create energy and support life. We may not be aware though that we are taking on the memory of what we ingest. Balanced health is dependent on eating real food and drinking pure water. It requires following the cycles of memory that align us with our true nature. It means nourishing ourselves for the light beings that we are.

In our day-to-day lives, we get caught up living through our experiences. We make food choices that align with our feelings and emotions. Our choice of food or drink triggers memory from past health responses and our body responds in alignment to the past frequency. It is our emotional responses that determine if our health will be adversely affected.

We are attracted to the frequency of a food in relation to our personal frequency. Prioritizing health is pushed aside in exchange for feelings of familiarity. We may be aware that what we are doing is unhealthy, but we do it anyway.

It brings us to a critical moment of recognition and familiarity. We can either make the transition to improve our health or stay in what we know.

We improve our health with the awareness of memory. In our awareness, we know that memory is transferred from food and drink into our being. We take on the memory of whatever we are eating, whether plant or animal, including the history of that species or of the synthetic man-made forms. Our being responds to memory with feelings and emotions based on our alignment.

Attaining balanced health requires eating and drinking for the memory of our being. We must aim to ingest balanced memory, as it will merge with our memory. Awareness of what is in our food or drink and its history will help us come into balance. Education on what we allow into our being has us making informed choices about our health. Our balanced health is in our power.

Our true nature beckons us to live according to the cycles of memory. It requires following the circadian rhythms of our planet and our bodies, as well as our personal life experiences. It includes eating and living with consistency while feeling the rhythm of balance as one with all life. It necessitates living in agreement with the cycles of memory to live in alignment with truth.

Nutrition goes beyond food and drink. We can consider taking in nourishment through sunlight, clean food and water, emotional balance, and living with gratitude. We can live true to the love that we are as one with all life. Being truly nourished is feeling life illuminated by the light that we are.

As beings of light, we depend on frequency to heal. We heal with frequency *as* nutrition. Our new focus can be on balancing our frequency to balance our health. Our quest for balanced health must transcend waiting for something outside of us to heal. We are powerful beings in our own right and we can heal through the light that we are.

Nutrition through balanced memory is the way to support life going forward. Healing relies on our awareness of what we ingest for nutrition to balance our memory. In our balance, we live through the cycles of memory in alignment with nature. We live nourished and in balanced health.

Memory Transfer

Everything in nature is an expression of memory. All beings are known to take in some form of nourishment to sustain life and then develop in response to the memory transferred. We ingest food and water to satiate hunger and thirst, but it is in our alignment to the transferred memory that we become nourished. Memory misaligned sustains fragmented memory.

Our choices of food and drink have a direct effect on our health. We chase poor quality foods and drinks as our minds align with fragmented memory. What we think is nourishment is often a misalignment of memory to sustain fragmentation for familiarity. We stay looped in fragmented memory and live in what we already know.

Our growth and development rely on intact healthy memory to support good health. Our health breaks down with the transfer of unhealthy memory. Plants and animals that developed with unhealthy and unethical treatments will undoubtedly transfer to us fragmented memory. We have to choose what nutrition we will allow to be transferred into our being.

Our being does not naturally align with man-made foods, supplements, and chemicals, yet there are fake processed foods being promoted, synthetic forms of nutrients that try and mimic true nutrition, and chemical particulates sprayed in our environment that all affect our health. Our beings are confused and have to work harder to bring memory back into balance.

Our imbalanced memory comes out in our emotions. We express outwardly in our actions the expression happening within. Nutrition comes in as memory and then is expressed as emotions showing us what is going on where we cannot see. We can clearly see through our emotions if balanced or adverse reactions are taking place in our health. Our emotions show us memory.

The transfer of memory of any kind interferes with our frequency. Our being resonates at a specific frequency for balance and is constantly correcting imbalances. Nutrients in alignment with our being sustain nourishment. Memory that is misaligned with our true nature interferes with our frequency and reinforces fragmentation.

In his book *The Healing Power of Water*, Masaru Emoto shows how information from the power of words and music imprint beautiful or unpleasant crystal images in water.[1] Our bodies are at least 70 percent water. The water we drink has memory of all the chemicals, drugs, plastics, and garbage that contaminate our waters. Memory *in* is information transferred.

Memory transferred for nutrition must be ingested with good intentions for balanced health. We can do our best to ingest the cleanest natural foods and pure water for sustenance. We can grow our own food and purify our water to ensure balance. Creating balance means being aware of what and how we eat and drink so we can transfer good intentions of peace, love, and gratitude into our being.

Nutrition is memory in alignment with our being. We are nourished by the food and water we choose in our response to the balance of our memory. The health of our memory is dependent on our emotional health. We support healthy memory with healthy choices and reinforce misalignment with poor choices. Memory aligned with truth sustains healthy memory.

Cycles of Memory

We are beings of memory that synchronize with the cycles of nature. Our alignment with the cycles of memory promotes good health, while disruption increases our risk for disease. Inconsistent diet and lifestyle habits affect the balance of our being. Our balanced health depends on living consistent with the cycles of memory.

We are rhythmic beings. We are healthiest when we wake up with the light of the sun and sleep in the dark of the night. We are a society that lives dominated by habits and daily routines that go against our circadian rhythms. Our bodies become confused with fluctuating habits and, consequently, our health suffers. The memory of our being gets disrupted.

Inconsistent sleep routines adversely affect our health. Poor sleep leads to craving sweets and unhealthy carbohydrates. Sugar imbalances affect our emotional state and we are led down a path of repeating poor habits to satisfy the disruption of memory. A consistent sleep routine is vital to all cycles of memory.

"It is now widely accepted that a functional and well-aligned circadian clock promotes [good] health, while circadian disruption increases disease risk."[2] Common diseases with an increased risk include psychiatric neurodegenerative, metabolic and cardiovascular disorders, immune system dysfunction, and some types of cancers.[3]

A large epidemiological Nurses' Health Study showed that cancer is associated with shift work and circadian rhythm disruption with an increased risk of dyslipidemia, hypertension, type 2 diabetes, heart attacks, multiple sclerosis, and inflammatory bowel disease.[4] Sadly, manipulating cycles of light and dark and diet and fasting is needed to balance health.

There is interest in creating drugs to "drug the circadian clocks" in our bodies.[5] Using drugs to manipulate cycles that are out of alignment with nature is not the answer to true health. Manipulation leads to more health concerns in a never-ending cycle of drugging a symptom to fix a problem. The problem lies in our unawareness of the true nature of our being.

Balanced health is in learning the rhythms of our bodies and staying true to them. Knowing how our rhythms can be used to our benefit brings us closer to balance. Women are blessed to have menstrual cycles that indicate balance or imbalance in their entire system and we can all see inconsistencies in our digestion. Knowing opens us up to true healing.

To be out of alignment with our cycles of memory affects the memory of all. The memory of our being knows there is misalignment with the rest of our world. The balance or imbalance of one is shared with all. True balance means to eat, drink, and take care of our health for the sake of the entire universe. It means nourishing our health because we are beings of collective memory.

We are beings of memory entrained with the cycles of nature. Our personal health relies on our alignment with circadian cycles. To live against the rhythm of nature is to support the risk of disease and poor health. Living nourished and in balance is to live with consistent healthy diet and lifestyle habits. It is to live true to the cycles of memory.

Nutrition for Light Beings

If we are light beings, do we even need to consume food in this dimension of awareness? It is well known that we can go without food, but not water. As beings of light, our healing is dependent on balancing our memory through frequency. Nutrition is based on our alignment in frequency with our choice of nourishment. True health is being nourished through our alignment with truth.

Our true nature has been forgotten in this fast-paced world. We make food choices based on the fastest options available, putting true nutrition aside. We consume fake foods and long-named, hard-to-pronounce preservatives while replacing water with sugared, caffeinated, and alcoholic drinks. True nutrition is nourishing ourselves for the light beings that we are.

The balance of our being depends on pure water and drinking a lot of it. We are at least 70 percent water and cannot live without it, yet most people do not get enough of it. Water is so important to the survival of our bodies that are needed to carry us through life. It is pure water that is free of chemicals, as well as toxic memory, that can help to bring us into balance.

As beings of light, we heal through frequency. It is in our alignment with our nutrition choices, whatever the diet preference, that we create balance within. Our memory becomes fragmented when the entire memory of our being is not in alignment with what we consume. The memory of our being recognizes misalignment and results in imbalanced health.

Nutrition for a light being consists of taking in more light. It literally means taking in more light from the sun while also eating more greens that depend on the light of the sun. Nutrition for our being consists of exposure to light upon waking and taking in more light through the daytime hours. We are beings of light who need light to exist.

Living as a light being is to be aware. It is to be aware of the memory and nutrient value of everything we consume. It is to be aware of how our food was grown and treated and what memory we are transferring into our being. Our awareness is vital to the balance of our being. In our awareness, we live balanced in our light.

In our light, we eat to sustain life—we don't live to eat. We know that everything we consume becomes part of who we are. Pure nutrition helps us navigate through this life in good health. We feel pure energy without the need for caffeine, sugar, or empty carbohydrates to get us through a day. To live as the light that we are is to live as happy, energetic beings.

Living in our light means being nourished in truth. We stand in our truth at all times and make nutrition choices based on truth. We eat with healthy intentions to promote balanced health. We prepare our food, salivate in its preparation, and chew with healthy intent while also being grateful and enjoying the entire process. We can then shine our light through balanced health.

To live in the light that we are is to live in the awareness of our light. It means eating and drinking for the nutrition and memory of our being. We make health choices that are in alignment with our light as well as our truth in values. It is in our alignment that we are in peace. In our peace, our frequency is in balance and we live nourished as the light beings that we are.

CHAPTER 10

Toxic Memory

W E ARE A TOXIC society. Our bodies are overburdened by internal and environmental toxins. Our health suffers and we see the toxicity come through our emotions. We avoid emotional pain and fall into past patterns of memory. The burden becomes worse as we spread toxicity around and step into the toxic memory of others. Society is sleepwalking into an abyss.

Awareness is dampened by toxicity. We live with brain fog and make poor decisions when burdened with toxins. Our bodies are overloaded with chemicals that are ingested, injected, and sprayed. Our indoor and outdoor air is polluted. Yet the vast majority of people do not see the dangers. It is time to lift the veil.

Our bodies are overwhelmed with toxins. We consume chemicals in our foods and water and breathe in chemicals from our air. Our skies and waters are filled with nanoparticles of heavy metals from geoengineering that affect our health and the health of our planet.[1] Our waters and fish are polluted with pharmaceutical drugs.[2] We are flooded with toxic chemicals.

Our health suffers as our beings become inundated with toxins. We see the burden come through as cancers, heart damage, autoimmune diseases, and autism, while we live with harmful Wi-Fi all around us, amplifying existing toxicity.[3] We have to work extra hard to keep our health in balance due to the increased amounts of toxins allowed in this world.

Toxicity comes through our emotions, showing that our health is being affected. Our existing unresolved emotions intensify while our health concerns get worse. Our emotions are true indicators of our health within. Our health impacts how we feel emotionally and it is in our awareness that we recognize the healing that is needed.

We fall into past patterns of memory in the avoidance of our emotional pain. In our emotional struggles, our being recalls and aligns with past toxic health events. We see similar symptoms appear and more emotions flood in. Our health concerns escalate and we see more serious symptoms occur. It is our responsibility to recognize our imbalances so we can heal.

We are beings of frequency. Our frequency does not stay contained as a body with borders. The energy of our being spreads out beyond our physical bodies and is shared with our surroundings. We share our frequency signature with others in close proximity. Our being takes on the toxicity of others and becomes burdened. We must do our best to spread balance.

We are living in a toxic world. We can easily be pulled into a false narrative when we are not living in truth. Our thoughts influence our decisions for our health. In our unawareness, we can become toxic in our body and mind and share toxicity with others. We have the power to be healthy and heal the memory of our being. It is in our balance that we share balance.

Imagine a healthy society—a world with healthy food, water, air, people, and animals living in peace. Are we willing to do our part to contribute balanced health to lift the burden of toxicity? Memory is beckoning us to come home to ourselves as balanced peace. It is in our peace that we share balanced health. In our awareness, we heal and help uplift the collective.

Toxic Overload

Why do we go to extremes with our health? We watch minor symptoms become major diseases. We eat foods and drink beverages that we know are not good for us. We ignore warnings of external dangers to our health. It is only when we get a major diagnosis that our health gets our undivided attention. We wait until our beings are burdened with toxins.

If there is a major disease, there is toxicity. Our bodies become overwhelmed and alarming symptoms come rushing through. It is in these moments that we go all in on trying to reverse or heal what was an afterthought in its minor stage. Our bodies need healing attention before symptoms appear.

In our avoidance, we continue to do what we know is not good for us. The fast foods and drinks, the alcohol, drugs, caffeine, and the sugars and snacks remain staples, while symptoms tell us we are imbalanced. Our imbalances turn to toxicity as we deal with our emotional pain at another time. Our inaction further escalates poor health.

We may hear what could be affecting our health and brush it off in disbelief. We prefer to live with our current conveniences to not upset our daily routines. Coffee, fast foods, lack of exercise, toxic news, alcohol, and poor sleeping habits persist. Our routines remain, but so do our health symptoms.

In our complacency, our symptoms turn to major health concerns. Fear takes over and we rush to find healing. Sadly, it usually includes more chemicals, drugs, and cutting things out. We miss the opportunity to truly heal. It would make more sense to clear the existing toxicity in our bodies to create balance before minor symptoms become major. Why must we complicate life?

The overload of toxins in our bodies seen as symptoms is a signal to get into balance. It is a warning sign to clean up the toxins in our life. Unhealthy foods and drinks, perfumes, toxin-coated cooking pans, and chemicals from dryer sheets burden our bodies and the environment. It is in our control to balance our health and help lift the collective toxic burden.

Our current balance or imbalance determines our strength in the face of toxins. The level of burden in our bodies will be the deciding factor for how sick we become from toxins that we encounter. A body overburdened with toxins cannot handle any more toxins. It is in our recognition of our imbalances that we can begin to heal.

Healing begins with seeing our health as our first priority. We need balanced health to navigate through life. It is up to each of us individually to take the initiative to clear the toxins from our lives. We forget the true nature of our being and get caught in a toxic trap. Healing happens with small steps toward balance.

We do not have to go to extremes with our health. We can clear up symptoms as soon as we are aware. We can eat foods and drink beverages that we know are good for us. We can be aware of toxic chemicals that are a danger to our health. We can live healthy lives by giving undivided attention to our health. We can live in balance and free of the burden of toxicity.

Toxic Recall

Why do we see recurring health patterns? We think we have healed and moved past a tragic health event, then it comes rushing through again. Our unresolved emotions align us with similar events of the past and toxicity begins to bubble up to the surface. We see similar health symptoms as our emotions get fueled once again. Our memory goes into toxic recall.

The memory of our being is always trying to balance out imbalances. Our memory recognizes fragmentation to create balance while our minds stay in alignment with past fragmented frequency. In the recognition of our imbalances, we can balance the memory of our being. We can prevent health patterns from reemerging.

We breathe a sigh of relief when we believe we have healed but then go back to the same ways of living. The same diet, relationships, and emotional expressions stay part of our daily routine, without recognizing what previously affected our health. We stay with only what we know. It is in the not knowing of our health causes that we leave an opening for our being to recall past toxic events.

Unresolved emotions keep us tied to fragmented frequency. Avoiding healing our emotions leaves the potential to activate past memory for similar symptoms to appear. Unresolved emotions align with past health events that create toxicity in our bodies. It is when we transform our emotions that we see our health transform. We balance our memory.

To see similar past health symptoms shows an emotional attachment to the associated frequency. We are in alignment with the emotions surrounding our health concerns. There has to be ground for the toxicity to develop in order for our bodies to recall past toxic health events. It is when we are already imbalanced that an emotion will activate what was lying in waiting.

Health symptoms come in with force to get our attention. Our minds seem to push our unresolved emotions aside, but our being remembers it all. We cannot fool memory. Our bodies will go into toxic recall of past health events whether or not our minds are aware of what is happening. We will see similar symptoms as our being recalls and is in alignment with the past frequency.

Our bodies remember toxic health events for our protection. It is within the nature of our bodies to respond rapidly to previously encountered health dangers. Memory shows signs and symptoms as it is trying to come back into balance. If ignored, symptoms will turn into greater health concerns. It is up to us to look, listen, and feel for what memory is trying to convey.

Our memory goes into toxic recall when it is overwhelmed. We see major symptoms and disease diagnoses long after memory has been activated. Autoimmune diseases and cancers do not show up instantaneously without gradually trying to get our attention with symptoms. Balanced memory is in our peace. Balanced health comes through our balanced memory.

We can live free of toxic health patterns. To live in balanced health is to be established in the peace of our being. We align with the frequency of peace, not tragedy. We live emotionally grounded in calm and past tragic health events are healed in the knowing of our true nature. Toxic health patterns cannot live in our peace. We live in the balance of our memory.

Toxic Communication

Language is a form of communication to help us navigate through life and bring us into balance. As our physical selves, we have learned how to communicate with words, but our beings use various types of communication along with words, such as sound, frequency, emotions, and other expressions. It is when we communicate imbalance that we spread toxicity.

We speak language that we learn though life and put sentences together without truly knowing the meanings of the words. We send out negativity without even knowing it. Slang like *my bad* is literally telling our being that we are bad and it is also sending that into the collective to say *all* is bad. We can make it a habit to say "peace and love" to negate negativity.

We are beings of light and we communicate through frequency. It is a form of communication that we may not visually see, but it is felt and known in depth. The frequency of our being as memory extends out around us and we can share toxic communication just by being in the vicinity of another. To be a balanced being is to also send out balance.

Emotions and other expressions help us express our feelings and understand others better. Anger, hatred, nonforgiveness, living in shame, not being grateful, and being focused on greed and fears communicate toxicity. In our toxic expressions, our being recalls past toxic events and we stay looped in struggle. We create restriction in our bodies that affects our health.

Toxic communication adversely affects our being. We see imbalances in our health and, when toxic, it becomes a challenge to access our words and memory. Our fragmented memory sends out symptoms as an alarm to get our attention. We share the balance or toxicity of our being with all. We have a responsibility to balance our health to communicate balance.

Communication through expressions helps us to know if we are safe around of others. Our facial expressions, body movements, and gestures are all signals to others we encounter. We express ourselves in ways that convey the frequency of our being. It is through our expressions that we communicate peace, not harm.

We resonate with sound as communication with our being. We feel negativity from discordant music and tones of voice. Attraction to cacophonous sounds is an indicator that we are trying to stay in a toxic frequency to be in familiarity. Harmonious sounds can help bring us back to the true nature of our being to resonate with peace.

Language is for us to share peace and love and help us remember our true nature. Communicating toxicity keeps us and the entire collective stuck in a loop of toxic communication. We have forgotten the trueness of language with possibly Sanskrit being the only to still hold true meaning. Communicating negative language aids toxicity, not peace.

Toxic language makes life difficult and keeps us from being in the peace of our true nature. Toxic communication affects our health and keeps us in a cycle of pain and suffering. Our words and other expressions matter to convey peace, not toxicity. In peace, we communicate and share peace.

CHAPTER 11

Fitness and Memory

How do our bodies remember fitness? Is there a correlation between current and past fitness? We push ourselves to follow diet, exercise, and lifestyle protocols only to fail in our attempts and then feel defeated. We get stuck in our emotional pain and poor fitness. In our alignment with memory, we can reach balanced and true fitness.

Fitness is often only thought to mean having a physically fit body. We seek out exercise programs with a goal to look like someone from a marketing picture while we miss the bigger picture. True fitness is in the balance of our physical, mental, emotional, and spiritual ways of being. We feel balanced in all areas of our being.

Our beings remember what is true to memory. All fitness that is not in line with balance will show as not working for us. To align with an imbalanced state of fitness will only bring up indicators to get our attention. We see health symptoms, as well as life struggles, as being able to help us move toward a healthier way of being. Our beings remember in our alignment.

To be in balance is to be in line with true fitness. It is to be aligned with the activities we are performing. Our misalignment to our fitness plans signifies a conflict within and divergence from the true nature of our being. We align with fragmented memory for familiarity and stay in an imbalanced fitness state.

Our true fitness potential goes beyond what can be imagined. We can certainly repeat a past state of fitness, but we can also connect with collective memory to reach a state that we have not accomplished before. All states of fitness require us to be in alignment with the memory of fitness for it to be established. Our thinking clouds our fitness goals and affects our potential.

We may wonder what links current to past fitness states. Our emotions initiate our actions and, when unresolved, our expressions are repeated. We choose similar fitness goals to aid our current emotions and have similar outcomes. It is the frequency that we are that aligns us with the memory of past fitness.

Our bodies respond to our alignment with memory. We see body composition changing whether we exercise or do no exercise. It is our alignment with the activity or lack of action that our bodies respond to with visible changes. We literally get to see the results of our alignment to memory. We see how our alignment matters to our health.

We are in constant reaction to memory. Our overall fitness is our response to our emotions and frequency. In our awareness, we can override poor decisions. We can see what is needed to be in balanced fitness and follow through for it to be established in our lives. If we are in constant reaction to unresolved emotional memory, then our emotions need to be balanced.

Our fitness is reliant upon our emotions. We are aligned with memory as the frequency that we are. In our balanced emotions, we live through the balance of our being. We only perform activities that we are in alignment with and experience no failure or defeat. We live in balanced fitness and memory.

True Fitness

We all long for a balanced state of fitness. We too often stop short of total balance. We get stuck in our routines that support our imbalances and lose sight of what can bring us into balance. Our short- and long-term goals often miss the demand needed to achieve balanced health, or we get too eager and burn ourselves out. It leaves us wondering: "What is true fitness?"

True fitness is to be in a health state that allows us to live a life filled with activities that we enjoy and to have the ability to perform them. We achieve better fitness through a healthy nutrition and exercise plan in which we align. We work on our emotions, practice gratitude and peaceful thinking. Our total memory is in balance in true fitness.

Total balance is often pushed aside to keep our habits in place. We focus on one area of fitness and leave the others behind. We believe that when we feel better from the one area of fitness, then we will tackle the hard-to-give-up habit. It seems to never work out that way. True fitness can only happen when we focus on *all* areas of fitness.

Our short- and long-term goals are dependent on our alignment to them. In our misalignment, we make excuses and focus on our limitations. We stay stuck in our emotional pain, even when unaware. Are we willing to face the truth and resolve unresolved emotions to align with true fitness? Amazing objectives have been achieved in the alignment of a goal.

True fitness requires effort. In our effort, we can enjoy a healthy life. The elderly can live non-assisted and autonomously, while reaping the benefits of strength and balanced health. Diseases fall away in exchange for overall balance and being over- or under-weight would not fit into our lives. True fitness is available to us.

Poor fitness affects the memory of our mind. Research indicates that exercise can generate new neurons and improve cognitive function in the hippocampus, which is the part of the brain involved in memory.[1] Fitness affects the memory of our mind but also the entire memory of our being. We can enhance our memory through a balanced fitness plan.

A balanced fitness plan has us feeling truly alive. We feel pure energy from true fitness that is unmatched by stimulants. Caffeine negatively affects our nervous system and robs the body of water, nutrients, and sleep while leaving people exhausted in the morning, reaching for their next fix. In our balance, we reap the benefits of true fitness.

In true fitness, we respect our bodies. We take care to live free of extreme fitness plans, just as we make sure to have a fitness plan. Our exercise programs are balanced with recovery plans and we also give our minds rest after intense mental work. We keep our emotions in check and we make sure to align with what brings us joy. We live in true fitness.

True fitness is available to all of us. It requires peace of mind and perseverance to be in balance. We do what it takes to support true fitness rather than support our imbalances and limitations. We make goals that respect our body, mind, emotions, and memory. We make our health our number one priority, knowing that in our balance, we are in true fitness.

In Line

Our being aligns with the memory of fitness to remember. Our fitness potential goes as far as our alignment. Our overall fitness, exercise, nutrition, and mental activity plans align with the memory of our personal past and the collective memory performance. In our alignment, we stand true to our tasks to be in line with the memory of fitness.

Our alignment with the memory of fitness is vital for an optimal outcome. We align with memory created from a particular task, whether we performed it or not. To not be in alignment with our chosen path will show as unsatisfactory results, or we will just not have the motivation to act on it. Our alignment to a positive outcome equals positive results.

It is our alignment to our fitness routine that matters above all. Everything else falls into place when we align with our goals. Otherwise, a desired goal stays a desire. Lack of movement shows that what we want is to actually stay in our familiar frequency, which only gives us a false sense of security. It is in our alignment with progress that we see progress.

Our mind and the memory of our being both need to be in alignment with the memory of fitness to see results. We are memory in form and it is the frequency that we are that is in alignment with what we are doing in every moment, whatever the activity. Potential in fitness is always there as we align with the collective memory. The memory of fitness always remembers.

Our fitness possibilities are hindered by our destructive mental activity. Our mindset gets looped into emotional attachments to our beliefs and we stay in alignment with poor lifestyle habits. Our potential will only go as far as our alignment and it is up to us to balance our imbalances. All is possible when we align with balanced memory.

In our balance, we make no excuses. We align with our fitness goals and make them work. We see health as a top priority and a foundation for everything that we do in life. To cheat our health is to suffer the consequences of a poor quality of life. Our overall fitness suffers and we stay aligned with poor fitness. In our alignment with truth, we live with optimal fitness.

In our alignment with true fitness, our fitness plans seem to line up perfectly with what we need for balance. The memory of fitness expresses itself as good results in our health. We make better decisions in our life and live in balance. In our balance, we feel physically and mentally fit and are able to enjoy life. We align with balanced fitness.

We are sentient beings of memory in biological form. Memory is frequency and it is the frequency that we are aligned or resisting that shows our fitness. Our minds seem to get in the way of our plans too often. It is in the alignment of our mind, biological being, and total memory that we live in harmony. It is to stand in our truth to be in line with true fitness.

Our being is always in alignment with the memory of fitness. The type of fitness that we align with is correlated to our frequency. We align with the fitness of our past or with others who did the same. We are always in alignment with what we are doing, no matter the activity. It is in our alignment with balanced memory that we are in line with true fitness.

Fitness and Emotions

Our emotions show through our fitness activity or as lack of interest. Many feel trapped in a body that is a different weight, size, or build than they desire and fight to even try to work toward balance. We become one with poor fitness in alignment with struggle. We stay in a loop of poor fitness to aid our emotional pain. Our fitness potential is tied to our emotions.

How do we disentangle ourselves from the grips of emotional pain? Our emotional attachments affect every aspect of our lives. Emotions impact our fitness decisions and our health in turn impacts our emotions. Our fitness suffers because of our unresolved emotions. Our fitness goals depend on our clarity, honesty, and alignment with optimal fitness.

Our goals need our alignment for success. We say willpower is needed to get motivated, but what is seen is a short burst of energy, which does not last. Our emotions kick in again, along with a nutrient or chemical signaling a need, so then we eat the cake, drink the caffeine or alcohol, smoke the cigarette, or do the drug. The willpower is gone, and we are hooked again.

We become one with poor fitness. A lack of interest in realizing balanced fitness can be traced back to our unresolved emotional pain. We find excuses and hold ourselves back or start a routine and fall right back into old familiar ways. We struggle to finish what we start. We live in conflict with our desired goals and our emotional attachments.

We feel trapped in a body that our thoughts try to reflect differently. We think back to times that we were fitter or dream of what could be without taking action. Our dreams stay stagnant while we align with the emotions that are in opposition to our desires. We are drawn to the frequency of familiarity without even being aware.

Emotions and our fitness potential are tied together. We live through the memory of our emotions and act out the frequency that we are. We eat or train less or more, depending on our alignment to memory in every moment. Our actions display for us the frequency that we are acting out. We are memory in form.

Our fitness improves with clarity of mind. Toxic buildup in our mind and body will show through our overall fitness as brain fog and lack of motivation. Toxic lifestyle and nutrition habits keep us stuck in an emotional loop and our fitness suffers. We live according to how we feel but miss that connection. Our emotions take precedence and we continue to live through the fog of toxicity.

Emotional well-being helps to balance all aspects of our being. In our search for true fitness, we try to find it through ways that change our body composition. We start vigorous exercise and nutrition plans with the goal to change how we look. Our goals lack the understanding of our search, which is to come home to the true nature of our being.

The deep knowing of true fitness brings a different focus to our plans. We know that all areas of fitness fall into place as we align with our true nature. Our emotions come into balance and we become one with true fitness. We live through the peace of our being and align with fitness as we stay in peace. In our emotional balance, we live in balanced fitness.

CHAPTER 12

Sleep and Memory

WHEN OUR BODY GOES to sleep at night, the memory of our being does not go away. Our memory is constant and is always balancing, whether we are awake or sleeping. Sleep is a vital way for our bodies to heal as well as work through unresolved emotions through our dreams. Missed sleep affects the memory of our being. Without sleep, memory fragments.

We need consistent sleep to revitalize. Sleep is the one necessity that cannot be traded for something else to take its place without major consequences. Our bodies cannot function optimally with poor sleep. The memory of our being is constantly trying to balance the effects from lack of sleep. In its absence, our bodies suffer and break down.

Missed sleep affects our overall health. Lack of sleep has us reaching for foods, sugar, and substances in our attempt to balance the demands of a body in distress. Erratic eating times and caffeine use further affect our sleep and health. Our entire circadian rhythm becomes disrupted. Consistency in sleep matters to balance our overall health.

We have all experienced or witnessed how our emotions affect our sleep. Our sleep affects our emotions and our emotions certainly affect our sleep. Without adequate sleep, we can find ourselves crabby and snapping at others. In times of emotional unrest, we stay up all night to think or worry. Our unresolved emotions affect all areas of our lives.

We even see our unresolved emotions come through our dreams. We try to work through our emotions through our dreams as we take part of a creation of scenes of people, places, things, and events. We cleverly connect with others of similar frequency and often bring our dreams to light in our waking hours. There are no coincidences in the healing of the memory of our being.

Sleep is vital to heal memory. We are memory in form and the memory of our being stays in resonance with fragmentation and fragments further without sleep. We use the memory of our minds to remember life events and our minds become foggy in the absence of sleep. Our bodies need sleep to repair and revitalize. Missed sleep fragments memory.

In our waking hours, we create the setting for our sleep. All our daily activities from the time of waking contribute to the quality of sleep we will get that night. The food we eat, caffeine we consume, and exercise we do or do not do all matter. A sleep routine to prepare us hours before bed is critical to get sufficient sleep, but our sleep routine starts upon awakening.

Memory heals or fragments through the day. Our memory balances in the healing of our bodies while our bodies heal in the balancing of memory. It is in our sleep that our bodies get to heal without the hindrances of the movement of our bodies and digestion of food. It is in our control in how we plan the activities through our days for us to get good sleep at night.

Memory is constant and needs sleep for balance. In our sleep, we heal. As we fall asleep the day may come to a close, but our beings are always working toward balance. Our bodies need rest to heal from all of what we put them through during the day, while our unresolved emotions get worked out through our dreams. With sufficient sleep, memory heals. *We* heal.

Revitalize

How many people truly feel revitalized after sleeping? We tip the scales so far off-balance with our daily activities that it is difficult to get back to center. Our sleep gets disrupted even without us being aware and we see our lack of sleep in our slow performance the next day. The purpose of sleep is to cleanse and heal. Our bodies go to sleep to revitalize.

Sleep is vital for our healing. We need sleep for the healing of our bodies and the memory of our minds and beings. Sadly, many people do not get the sleep they need to truly revitalize and instead wake up feeling unrested with the desire to stay in bed. So many people are walking around half-asleep. It becomes normal to not remember feeling revitalized.

Our bodies adapt to their own sleep rhythm. We get in our routines and our bodies fall into alignment over time. We may adapt to schedules, but our sleep is still disrupted from not being in alignment with the true circadian cycle. Our health shows us the disorder that is happening inside our bodies. Our bodies need consistent sleep.

To go against memory begs compensation. We can only borrow against our energy for a short time before we see health consequences. Our health depends on us to respect the true nature of our beings. Disrupted sleep rhythm depletes us and fragments memory. We move further away from being revitalized. It is memory that begs us to come back to balance.

Our daily activities matter for balanced sleep. We feed our poor sleep imbalances with poor diet and exercise habits. We crave carbs and sugar and eat late at night, burdening our digestive system in its healing phase. Some people over-train with exercise, while others lay stagnant. Either way, sleep becomes further disrupted. We get stuck in a cycle of poor sleep.

We may not even be getting the sleep that we *think* we are. The amount of time in bed does not always equal the amount of sleep we get. It is estimated that as many as seventy million people in the United States have a sleep disorder, which includes many conditions that negatively affect sleep.[1] We need quality sleep for our bodies to heal.

Our bodies need sleep at night to cleanse. It is in our sleep that metabolic waste is swept from our brains through the glymphatic system. "The glymphatic system plays a key role in regulating directional interstitial fluid movement, waste clearance, and, potentially, brain immunity."[2] Sleep is vital for our healing.

Our health depends on us taking control of our sleep. It is important that we understand the causes of sleep disruption to take action before we see health concerns. Drinking alcohol and caffeine and eating late at night disrupt sleep. Our understanding of how substances, foods, and activities affect our sleep help us bring balance to our sleep.

We have the power to feel revitalized after sleeping. We can change sleep statistics if we make sleep a priority. Awareness in our waking hours helps us know that all our decisions affect the sleep we will get that night. We know that the purpose of sleep is to cleanse and heal. Our bodies go to sleep at night to revitalize.

Emotional Memory and Sleep

We take our unresolved emotions with us into our sleep state. The imbalanced emotional memory of our being shows through our sleep patterns. We lay awake at night to think and worry, only to feel worse the next day. Our missed sleep affects our overall health, but we repeat the cycle anyway. Our unresolved emotional memory takes control of our sleep.

We are not free of suffering when we fall asleep. Our beings are always working through memory to heal. In our sleep, memory consolidates and organizes. We need sufficient sleep to heal so we can be more attentive in our waking hours. Our sleep gets disrupted if we allow our emotions to take hold of our being. In our suffering, we do not sleep in peace.

Our suppressed emotions during the day lead to poor sleep at night. In our waking hours, we live through our emotional memory and make decisions based on our emotions. We get caught in habitual behaviors that affect our ability to sleep and then our poor sleep further affects our health. Our emotions increase our risk for health symptoms to arise.

Poor sleep adversely affects our overall physiology. Lack of sleep negatively affects our metabolism, appetite regulation, and the functioning of brain, immune, hormonal, and cardiovascular systems.[3] Sleepiness and the inability to focus have led to car accidents as well as mood, memory, psycho-social concerns, and deficits in performance.[4] We *need* sleep.

Unresolved emotions have us living in fragmented emotional memory. We lock in how we feel and limit ourselves from opening up to healing. Our limitations are obstacles in our waking hours and impair the ability of our bodies to heal in our sleep. We live looped in our suffering with our memory repeating the same healing. Memory heals when emotions are resolved.

Memory continues to be fragmented in our suffering. We miss sleep to stay awake and suffer in our reflections. Our thoughts and feelings shroud our true nature as we get caught in the painful events of our lives. We go over memories as we forget the peace of our true nature. In the overlooking of our truth, we lay awake and suffer.

Our sleep is so important to the balance of our mood. Missed sleep can lead to imbalances that can literally feel like a state of depression. Moodiness keeps us in resonance with past emotional memories of similar feelings. Lack of sleep can lead to emotional and mood disorders.[5] Sleep balances mood and memory.

Emotional memory and sleep are tied together in our healing. We need sleep to heal emotional memory and bring a new beginning to the day. Our thoughts and feelings tend to pull us right back to where we were before sleep and have us going over the same experiences with the same mindset. We have an opportunity every day to wake and start anew.

We can heal our emotions and bring peace with us into our sleep state. We will see our balanced emotional memory come through our sleep as we rest well and dream in pcace. In our waking hours, we feel well rested with clarity of mind and a balanced mood. We see our overall health in balance. We reap the benefits of taking control of our emotions and sleep in peace.

What Is a Dream?

A dream is made up of frequencies that take form as characters and scenes. The characters we see are representatives of the frequency that we align with. Our unresolved emotions come through in our engagement with similar frequencies of minds and activities to help us heal. In our dreams, we work through emotional memory free of interference. We dream to heal.

Pure conscious awareness illuminates our emotional memory as dreams. We see our emotional memory come to life as we travel through a world that seems so real. Our dreaming minds sort through our emotions with symbols and representations to bring balance to the memory of our being. We see our thoughts, feelings, and emotions illuminated in our dreams.

At the border between sleep and wakefulness, our dreams are clear. It is in that moment that we can grasp the visual content and feelings from our dreams. In our sleep, our minds work to consolidate our emotional memory, but we can incorporate our healing into our waking hours by learning to interpret the meanings of our dreams. Clarity turns into healing.

In our dreams, we engage with similar frequencies of minds to find balance. The memory of all individual minds works together to create balance for the whole. We are a microcosm of the macrocosm. In our dreams, we drop any animosity held for others and work together for healing. The healing of one is the healing for all.

The people, objects, and places in our dreams are depictions of frequency. The arguments or disturbing content are only the emotional workings of our individual minds, not relating to the literal people, places, or objects in the dream. Prophetic and lucid dreams represent a strong and flawless alignment to the frequency that we are working through. It is all frequency.

We all dream. Some people say they do not remember dreams, while others take part in their dreams and change the events as they develop. Our ability to remember our dreams ties into many factors, such as imbalances in our emotions or biology, as well as eating late and burdening our digestive system. Our health and daily activities become part of our dreams.

Recurring dreams are indicating complex unresolved emotions that need healing. The reappearance of past dream settings and characters is a realignment with that frequency, whether it is pleasant or disturbing. Identifying and working through the emotions that underlie our dreams can heal the associated fragmented emotional memory.

The memory of our being knows where we need balance. The content of our dreams is a visual as to what healing is taking place. The remembrance of our dreams gives us a clue into what we may miss or try to suppress in the avoidance of our emotional pain. We cannot suppress emotional memory. Our memory does not go away in our sleep or dreams.

We go on journeys every night to heal our being. In our dreams, we get to experience the diversity of the one collective mind that we share. We rest as emotional memory works through the light of our being in alignment with other frequencies. It is in our dreams that we are free to roam without the interference of our projected thoughts. In our sleep, we heal.

PART III

Emotional Transformation:
An Exploration to Transcend Emotional Pain

We are about to go on a healing journey that we cannot return from. Our thoughts and beliefs will be changed forever. We will be open to viewing the world in a whole new light. We will know at the depth of our being that we are in control of our evolution. We will see what aligns with truth and we will not go against ourselves. We are about to be transformed.

On our journey to open to our light we awaken to truth. It is in our truth that we are aware of our light and the light of others. We live true to our being and are guided by truth. In truth, we own our pain and live free of fears and suffering. We feel a deep sense of freedom as peace. It is truth that sets us free.

To be emotionally transformed is to live free of emotional suffering. Emotional transformation is not an end stage of enlightenment; it is an opening to live in awareness and constantly update our healing into our awareness. We end our emotional attachments and dissolve our ego identity as we know it. We live free.

In our emotional pain we live in restriction. Our entire being feels our unresolved pain that we have avoided in order to not feel. We find clever ways to distract while not knowing that it is *feeling* our pain that leads us to freedom. In our avoidance, we stay stuck in a loop of pain and struggle. We live clouded in darkness and suffer.

To live transformed is to open to the truth of awareness. In our awareness, we awaken to what truth is and is not. We clearly see our thoughts and beliefs change as we step out of the known. We live emotionally aware and in peace. We see that our true awareness is the awareness of all, and we live in the power of that knowing.

Transforming our emotional pain is to stand in our truth as power. In our power, we see past our ego identity, name, and form. We know that power is not based on external strength or societal status. In our truth as power, we live true to the light beings that we are. We live free of the ego-structures that restrict our freedom. In our truth, we live as one universal power.

Emotional transformation transforms us at the depth of our being. We feel freedom as forgiveness, gratitude, and love. Our hearts are open to feeling in connection with all life. In our freedom, we live in peace and in the flow of life. We only follow our inner guidance and live in the light of our truth. We feel true freedom.

To be emotionally transformed is to live as the light that we are. In our light, we live free of emotional attachments and fears that restrict our freedom. We feel universal unity, one with the light of others. In our light, we feel the love that we are and extend light as love to all. We live united in light as the light beings that we are.

Emotional transformation is a lifelong journey. We will continue to heal, no matter our past openings to truth. In our continued healing, we break through barriers to our freedom. To be emotionally transformed is to stand in our truth. We live true to our being and are guided by the light that we are. We are about to come home to ourselves.

CHAPTER 13

Into Awareness

WE START OUR EMOTIONAL healing journey stepping into awareness. We ground ourselves in the present and see what is true and what is false. In awareness, we are able to stand calm in a heightened emotional moment knowing that we are not our pain. We expand our perception and see beyond the known. In our awareness, we awaken to truth and will not return to our slumber.

To open our awareness, we can ask the questions "Who am I?" and "Why am I here?" When the deep meaning of our existence is considered, we find that there is more to life than the superficial. We are here for a deeper purpose than we can humanly conceive. We are not just the physical bodies that we see. To be in awareness is to appreciate the depth of our being.

To be aware is to clearly see what truth is and is not. In our awareness, we see the truth of who we are with no effort. We see how our thoughts are constructed from our conditioning. We learn that our emotional pain is not what we think. The falsities of our conditioning and our known thoughts and suffering dissolve in the truth of our awareness. We live truth.

In our awareness, we are attentive to the truth. We question our limited known thoughts to see what is false. We expand our perception and see beyond the known to clearly see where we have been sleeping while awake. It is in awareness that we awaken to the truth. In our awareness, we see how the false cannot survive in truth.

To be aware is to be grounded, facing our emotions as they come. We see that our suffering lies in our attachments and that we are not our pain. We are able to feel our surroundings and inquire into a deep knowing that we do not need emotional attachments to feel safe or belong. In awareness, we feel safe and know we belong everywhere.

As we open to our awareness, we know that we are all one collective consciousness. We can hear the thoughts and feel the emotions of others far across the globe and beyond. Our receptivity allows us to be in unity with the entire collective that we are a part of. We see the fact that our personal thoughts and emotions affect everyone. We are awake.

To live awake is to know awareness in depth. To be aware is to know that we are more than our ego identity. We know that it is pure conscious awareness that is a witness to our experiences. It is to know that it is awareness that is aware. In the depth of awareness, we are open to viewing the collective as sharing one light as awareness.

In awareness we feel the love that we are. To be in awareness is to feel an infinite universal connection with no division, borders, or duality. Our feeling of love heals our emotional pain as we know it and we extend love to all.

In awareness, we feel immeasurable love because we know that we *are* love.

To step into awareness is to open to a depth of knowing. We see beyond our known perception and clearly see where we have been sleeping. We continue to stay open to seeing truth. We live in emotional peace and know that we are not our pain. It is in our awareness that we are awake.

Emotional Awareness

Awareness is essential in healing our emotions. We heal when we face and acknowledge our pain. To avoid our feelings is to stay in restriction and suffering. It is in our awareness that we must meet our pain and end our attachment. Emotional awareness dissolves our suffering. To face our emotional pain we must be aware of our emotions.

To be aware of our emotions is to be clear about what we are feeling and why. Awareness has us checking in with ourselves to assess our feelings. In the knowing of our emotions, we hear and feel into our thoughts and emotions before we respond with words or actions. We understand why we are feeling the way we are and respond from that knowing.

Our emotions are a part of every waking moment and our decisions are based on our emotions, whether joy or pain. When we are in awareness, we can breathe into the moment and then reflect on our feelings. In emotional awareness, our choices are made intentionally in whatever the circumstance. It is in our awareness that we can choose a grounded response.

In emotional awareness, we are grounded. We can open our hearts to others, especially while in a heightened emotional moment. Compassion takes our focus off ourselves and opens our heart to others. It is in our pain that we cannot see past ourselves. In our compassion, heightened emotions get diffused and we are grounded in love and calm. We stay aware.

As we stand in emotional awareness, relationships of all kinds flow and evolve. There is depth to a conversation, not just superficial words and responses. Our emotions remain calm as we feel heard and valued. Our words are not empty of meaning. We truly listen to others as they listen to us. We feel safe.

Feeling safe is critical to our emotional, as well as our physical, safety. Emotional cues on safety are so often ignored because many people are not clear on what is *not* emotionally safe. To know when we are emotionally *unsafe* is to feel into a deep knowing. We tend to become complacent with feelings of discomfort because they are familiar. Awareness leads to safety.

In emotional awareness, we discern what is underlying our feelings and emotions. We know if our short temper is from a sugar imbalance, lack of sleep, past emotional trauma, or all of them. We understand if our emotions are being activated from the facial expressions of another, a scent, a tone of voice, or an environmental setting. We see clearly in awareness.

In our emotional awareness, we clearly see our attachments connected to our pain. We are aware that our emotional attachments to people, places, things, events, traditions, and beliefs are an attempt to attain a sense of security. It is in the loss of an emotional attachment that we suffer. In our awareness, we see that our security is in the light of our truth.

In our emotional awareness, we face our pain and heal. We see that in our avoidance we stay in restriction and suffering. We see clearly that it is in our emotional attachments that we suffer. In our emotional awareness, we face our pain. We end our attachments and our pain, as we know it, dissolves. We see clearly in our emotional awareness and live in peace.

Perceptive Awareness

To be perceptually aware is to see what is beyond the visible. It is to know in depth what is beyond our understanding. We see past our known senses and open to a freedom that defies all conceptual limitations. Perceptive awareness is to have complete clarity to see the truth. We see truth and know it at the depth of our being.

Awareness, as seen through our perception, is unique only to us individually. It is our interpretation of what we outwardly experience through our senses and how we organize it. It is also how we interpret our surroundings through our mind. A mind in disorder will see chaos. It is in clarity through insight that we see truth. A clear perception is to see through a clear mind.

Perceptual awareness is seeing our universal connection. Our connection as one goes beyond a superficial saying. This is a fact that goes beyond humanity being one. We are all one conscious, universal mind. We are one with all life and everything surrounding. Expanding our perception helps to lift awareness universally.

Our perceptive awareness will only go as far as our limitations. Being perceptually aware is to break through our conditioning and see beyond our current thinking and believing. We all have the innate ability to be open and inquire into our shared universal mind. It is in our perceptive awareness that we embrace a truth beyond the limitation of thought as only being our one mind.

To see beyond our current perception is to end all attachments to known beliefs. We cannot open to the truth if we are following what others have told us is truth. In our awareness, we see truth. Our perception is distorted by what we already know and believe. Perceptive awareness is to know truth and to see truth in the freedom of that knowing.

In our awareness, our conditioning and ego-structures are held up to truth. We see the false in what has been considered truth. We know with depth what is distortion. We see how life is perceived through a lens of deception that hides the truth. The distractions that we used to hold our false security are no longer relevant. In our awareness, we see clearly.

As we expand our awareness, our psychological borders dissolve. We see a connection with all life across the universe and feel united as one. We see beyond our physical locality and know with depth that we belong everywhere and so do all other beings in this universe. We are all one. In our awareness, our hearts are open and the barriers that divide us are lifted.

In our awareness, we are open to viewing the world in a whole new light. Our perception shifts as we remain open to truth. We open to freedom as we transcend our conditioning and known thoughts. Life becomes effortless in our awareness. We remain open and free. It is in our awareness that we live free and in our light.

In our perceptive awareness, we see beyond the known. We live free of the limitations of conditioning and impurities of mind. We see connection instead of division and borders. We are open to seeing truth that can reveal the false in our current beliefs. In our awareness, we live with complete clarity in truth. We live by the light of our truth.

Sleeping While Awake

Are we truly awake to what is going on around us? Do we only follow daily routines and believe what we are told? Do we look beyond a narrative for truth? In awareness, we step out of what we currently see and know to awaken to an understanding that may be hard to see and hear. As we open our awareness, we can reflect on where we have been sleeping while awake.

To be aware of what we miss that is often right in clear view, we must ask questions and then more questions. We must question government and political entities, the media, and medical, financial, education, and religious systems. It is in our inquiry that we see manipulation and control for power. In our awareness, we see beyond the known.

We awaken to truth through discernment. We see beyond a narrative for what we have been told is true or false. We see past what divides us into thinking one way or another. We cannot see true from false if we are only listening to one side and that side is telling us what they think of the other side. In awareness, we do not take sides and we do our own research.

We are kept asleep through the suppression of information. We are led astray with disinformation. Our freedom is a threat to those in positions of power and we will be held back from our true potential only to advance greed. We must awaken to the truth of who we are and take control of our evolution. It is in our awareness that we are awake to the power that we are.

To be awakened to truth reveals the power within us to heal. We must ask why we are led to believe that we need poison under the guise of medicine for healing. Can the pharmaceutical drugs that the majority of people are told they need put them in a fog or have them sleeping while awake? It is in our awareness that we see control used to suppress our innate power.

Are we asleep to the truth of technology? In our awareness, we see past the new technology that will hinder our innate power and we also see the truth behind the antiquated. Is there a motive behind what is pushed as new or what has not advanced? Could control be under the appearance of innovation as well as stagnation? It is in our awareness that we know.

In our slumber, we follow and conform. We follow the mainstream narrative and conform to the societal standard. We give our power over to the control of others. We have to be willing to step out of the known and stand completely alone in a world that praises the adaptation to the known. In our awareness, we stand in our power.

In awareness, we see the power in unification. We heal ourselves and open our hearts. We stop fighting each other and unite for the healing of all. Healing humanity will open our hearts to other beings in this universe. In awareness, we see beyond the false narratives. It is in our awareness that truth and freedom are uncovered.

To be awake is to be aware of the truth. We step outside of the known and are able to see truth through all of the busyness of society. Truth opens up a world of wonder when we do not turn away out of convenience or complacency. It is in our awareness that we feel true freedom. Why would we want to stay in a slumber?

Awakened to Truth

We have stepped into awareness to see beyond the known. We are now aware of the truth that has been clouded in conditioning. We have opened to a freedom that is beyond our previous perception and understanding. We feel a depth of knowing that makes the superficial loud and clear. We live true to the truth. We are not sleeping. We are awake.

Our awakening to truth has us living in truth. We have opened our perception to see beyond the known and we now stay curious. It is in our awareness that true and false are clear. We see truth clearly and we will not return to the deception of conditioned thoughts and beliefs. We stay awake and live in awakened truth.

In our awareness, we act through the knowing of our awareness. We live aware of our thoughts, feelings, and emotions as we see beyond the limitations of a conditioned perception. We live in the knowing that we share our memory with others and our actions create balance or imbalance. To be awakened to truth is to live truth.

In our awakened awareness, we are emotionally aware. We live free of emotional attachments that lead to suffering. We hold no desires or expectations that only keep us bound to an outcome. We live emotionally balanced and flow with life. It is in our awakening to truth that we live emotionally aware, unrestricted.

Opening to truth lifts the veil of unawareness. We see clearly what was hiding behind the conditioning that is aimed at keeping us powerless and at the mercy of false power. We see that true power is within all of us. It is in our awakened truth that we know in depth that truth equals freedom. We live free of deception.

In our awareness, we live free of the divisive thoughts that keep us divided. We feel a connection to everyone and everything. To be awakened to truth is to see beyond the superficial and know that our thoughts, feelings, and actions are shared with the collective. We know unity in depth.

In our awareness, we feel genuine love and compassion. Our hearts are open and we feel a love that cannot be conceptualized. We feel a deep love for the entire collective and feel that we are safe, supported, and loved. It is in the truth of awareness that we know that love is not limited to someone or something. We *are* love.

Awakening to truth is freedom. We are not bound to an understanding that keeps us in suffering. It is a feeling that is not limited to borders of confinement. We live free of the restriction of emotional suffering and flow with life as experiences come and go. We live true to truth as we live aware of our true nature. We live awake.

In the truth of our awakened awareness, we see beyond the known. We stand in our awareness and live in true freedom. We live free of suffering and live in peace. Our perception is open and free to see beyond the superficial. In our awareness to truth, we live with open hearts with love for all. It is in this freedom that we are truly awake.

CHAPTER 14

Owning Our Pain

To own our pain is to stand in truth. In our truth, we do not defy the true nature of our being or what we value. We become one with peace, not struggle; health, not illness; harmony, not conflict. We stand in our truth and power and transform blame and division into ownership and unity. We stay consistent with who we truly are and we heal in the light of our truth.

To heal emotional pain is to own our feelings, emotions, and actions. We hold ourselves accountable for our feelings, no matter the circumstance. We take control of the decisions we make and own the feelings around what may have happened to us that was out of our control. We know that we are in charge of our feelings and emotions.

We own our pain when we stand in our truth. In our truth, we heal. We stay consistent with what aligns with our truth as well as our values. In our truth, there is no suffering. We see the falsity of our emotional attachments and end them. We see that we are not only our body and mind and we live from the light of our truth. To stand in truth is to not go against ourselves.

In the defiance of our truth, we see adversity in our lives that relates to living inconsistently with our truth. Defying our truth leads to conflict and suffering with a victim mindset. We feel victim to circumstance and use blame as justification. Owning our pain leads to living free of pain and suffering. We live true to ourselves.

In truth, we become one with health, not illness. To heal our health is to know that there are unresolved emotions underlying our health concerns and that these emotions are ours to transform. Our emotions impact our health, and our health further impacts our emotions. Owning our health is to own our pain and to know that we are not in a fight against ourselves.

As we stand true to who we are, we become one with peace, not struggle. Our struggles dissolve as we take ownership of our lives. We live free of the fears that hold us back. We feel peace. It is in our peace that we know we are living in truth. To live in struggle is to live powerless. To own our pain is to feel true power.

To own our pain is to stand in our power. We learn that our personal power is not based on external strength or a facade. In our power, we do not stand alone in pain and separation; we transform division into unity and separation into connection. We know that our power is the power of all. It is in our power that we own our pain and stand united with all.

As we own our pain, we live in harmony. We live from our truth and feel in balance. We feel no desire to blame, as we see no fault. We own our pain because it is ours. We stand united with the entire collective and in harmony as one. We see conflict as going against truth. Owning our pain is to live balanced and flow with life.

We own our pain as we see truth. We see the false in what was considered true. We stand in truth and we do not go against ourselves. In our truth and power, we turn pain into true love, illness into balanced health, and victim mentality into power. We feel connected and in peace. We stand in our truth and power and our pain dissolves in the light of our truth.

Standing in Our Truth

To own our pain is to stand in the truth of who we are. We live in alignment with the true nature of our being, as well as our personal truth. In our truth, we own our pain and live free of emotional attachments and suffering. We live in the flow of life and recognize resistance as going against truth. We stand in our truth knowing that it is our guiding light.

To be true to who we are is to first know who we are. We have been conditioned to take on the beliefs of our parents, caregivers, teachers, preachers, doctors, and other significant figures in our lives. So many of us are walking around running a program that is not true to who we are. To stand in truth is to see the false in what was thought to be truth.

Standing true to conditioned beliefs comes with judgment. We get caught in a labeled box of what society considers truth and hold ourselves up to a false standard. We feel demoralized if we fail while following a laid-out path of success. We have to ask ourselves if we truly align with that path or if we are following societies definition of success. In our truth, we do not follow.

Standing in the truth of who we are is to step into our power. We feel power that is not defined by external strength. Our true power is not based on selfishness, dominance, or control. In our truth, our power radiates from the light that we are. We stand in truth to contribute to lifting the power of the collective. Our power is the power of all.

To stand in truth is to stand united as one. Our ultimate truth stands for who we truly are as one conscious awareness. Staying true to our true nature allows us to feel our oneness with all life. When we stand in the truth of who we are, we only attract truth back to us. We are in alignment with our relationships, work life, and where we live. We live truth.

Truth is order in alignment with the true nature of our being and our values. We stand in truth and we do not fight against ourselves. In our truth, there is no conflict because we see resistance as going against our truth. We stand in our truth knowing that it guides us on a true path. In our alignment, we live a life that flows.

In truth there is freedom. We are free of the limitations of emotional attachments that lead to restriction and suffering. We clearly see the fears that lead us to suffer and our fears are diffused through truth. We stand in the freedom of our truth and know there is nothing to fear. It is in our truth that our pain is healed and we feel freedom. We live in peace.

In truth, we see distortion of thought clearly and are not led astray. We know there is no confusion in truth. We see the false in our troubled thoughts and end them. In truth, we live free of the duality of mind. We see connection where there was separation and unity where there was division. We transcend duality as we live in the light of our truth.

To stand in our truth is to be in alignment with truth and to allow the light of our being to shine. We own our pain and we do not suffer. We feel free of emotional attachments and allow life to flow. We stay consistent with our truth and live in balance. It is in our truth that we stand in alignment with the true nature of our being.

Defying Our Truth

To defy our truth is to be in a state of powerlessness. We see adversity in our lives that relates to being against who we truly are. We feel victim to our circumstance and use blame as justification. Challenges arise as we live outside of our truth and values. In our truth, we take ownership of our lives. In our defiance, we betray ourselves.

Defying our truth is to go against every part of the powerful being that we are. We take on a victim mindset and look for someone or something to blame for our challenges. We wait for something outside of us to change and stay stuck in our pain. We accept the false as truth and we stay in a state of powerlessness.

To defy our truth is to be aligned with the false. True power is replaced with a fight for external power and greed. False authority is accepted as truth and the disempowered get imprisoned in a lack mindset while chasing the false. We stay divided with who has more power from money and societal success. Truth and power cannot be attained through the false.

In the defiance of our truth, challenges arise to get our attention. We see challenges in our health, our social and intimate relationships, our work life, and where we live. We blame our experiences on people or events. We accept our lives as difficult as we exert more effort to escape our struggles. We lose control of our lives and defy the true nature of our being.

To go against our truth is a betrayal of the self. We deceive ourselves into believing what we are told is truth. Media and government become the authority over personal inquiry. Many accept being a follower as confusion and dissatisfaction increase. We go against ourselves when we do not inquire into what truth is or is not.

We see the defying of truth in our everyday lives. We work jobs that we hate or that are opposite to our values but feel there is no choice. We go forward with something that we do not believe in. We say yes when we mean no. We stay in relationships that do not share our same values and beliefs. We struggle immensely and wonder why life is so hard.

In the defiance of our truth, we fight against ourselves. We hold emotional attachments as truth and feel devastated by loss. We avoid facing our pain because it is too hard. We take the projected pain of others as truth of our imperfections while we omit seeing the false. We attach to our pain with false reason. It is in the defiance of our truth that we suffer.

To go against our truth is to go against the entire collective. In our defiance, we add to the growing conflict and become a limitation to universal freedom. We are one universal mind. In our truth, we take ownership of our lives and contribute to healing the collective. We see our healing as the healing of all. We see truth as freedom.

To free ourselves of our defiance, we must step into our power and take ownership of our lives. We inquire into our personal truth and stand true to that knowing. We see adversity as being inconsistent with our truth and we do not fight against ourselves. In our truth, we are in control of our lives and connect with the true nature of our being. Life flows and is in balance.

Owning Our Health

Owning our health means being empowered to live in balance. We live imbalanced when we feel victim to our health. We hurt our health when we accept that our body has failed us. We lose when we give our power over to someone else to heal us. To own our health is to know that we have an innate ability to heal. We heal when we become one with balanced health, not illness.

To own our health is to bring balance to every part of our being. We heal when we know that we are not only our physical body. Our biological, psychological, emotional, and spiritual parts all need attention to truly heal. Owning our health requires us to take the initiative to bring balance where it is needed and not become complacent with less than balance.

Owning our health has us standing in our truth and taking control of our lives. We look within for answers and do not wait for something outside of us to change. We follow our inner knowing and only take a healing journey that aligns with our truth. We heal when we embody the powerful beings that we are and know that we heal in the light of our truth.

To own our health is to not give our power over to persuasion and fear. We know that we are not a failing machine that needs intervention. Owning our health means inquiring within, without coercion, to find a healing path. In our fear, we step out of our power and allow our emotions to drive our decisions. We transcend fear in the light of our truth.

Our emotional health is vital to owning our overall health. Unresolved emotions keep us in a loop of emotional pain and health concerns. Our emotions impact our health, and our health further impacts our emotions. To heal is to step into our power and face the emotions underlying our pain. It is to resolve our unresolved emotions.

To own our health is to become one with balanced health, not illness. It is because of our emotional attachment that we lose our power. We become laser-focused on our pain. We become one with it. We become one with the name of a disease and try to heal it by its name. To truly heal is to end our emotional attachment to the name of a disease and become one with balanced health.

Owning our health is to be empowered. It is knowing that we are powerful beings and that balanced health is our right. To own our health is to be free to choose a healing path that aligns with our truth. It is to take our health seriously and not go against our truth. Owning our health gives us freedom to live balanced lives.

To own our health is to feel true freedom. We are free to live a life without restriction and suffering. We are not bound by the dictates of false authority. We are our own authority. We live by the truth of who we are and we do not go against ourselves. To own our health is to stand in our truth and power and live free.

Owning our health is to stand empowered. We feel empowered by knowing that we are not only our physical bodies and we have the innate ability to heal. In our power, we do not feel victim to our health. We initiate our healing and bring balance to every part of our being. We stand in our power, own our health, and heal in the light of our truth.

Standing in Our Power

To stand in our power has us radiating truth as power. We stay consistent with who we are and own our pain. We see clearly what is true or false and know that power is not based on external strength or societal status. We live as our own authority. We know that our power represents our truth and when we stand in the power of our truth, true power is reflected.

We see distortion of power as truth all around us. We are taught and shown that strength is a form of power. We see our past traumas turn into falsifications of power to mask our pain. We think we stand strong in the face of challenges only to feel defeated by nonfulfillment. False power is not sustainable—it collapses in the face of truth and shows up as adversity rises.

Life adversity wanes as we stand in truth as power for change. We do not wait for laws of equality, governmental change, fair distribution of wealth, and for everyone to come together for a common cause. We see our conditioned perception of being taught to stay in waiting. Our power is in this moment and we flow with change as we radiate our truth as power.

We stand in powerlessness when we hold on to pain. We are in a powerless mindset when we lose ourselves to ancestral, cultural, and historical pain. Our power is in healing our personal pain. Being angry about past events is not doing justice to who has come before us, who will come after us, or who we truly are in this moment: powerful beings.

Our power is in our connection. We heal individually and collectively when we see no opposing sides. We all have painful human stories, no matter the events of the past or who we have seen as an enemy. We are not categories in this interconnected web of life. We are separate only by our thinking minds. In our truth, we feel our connection and know we are all one.

To stand in our power is to know that there is no one above or below us. We grow and evolve when we know that we all have strengths and weaknesses. We all share painful human emotions with struggles. Our power is in our embrace of all our challenges and emotional pain. In our power, we know truth as power.

We stand empowered when we do the inner work. We are not in our power when we externalize our pain as blame or judgment. We hurt others and ourselves when we use control or power through aggression. We rob ourselves of power when we shut down from being vulnerable. True power is to own and heal our emotional pain and be the power that we are.

We stand in our power as our own authority. In our power, we do not follow those who claim authority. We listen to others with discernment and only take on what aligns with our truth. We know in depth what is best for our lives, and we do not go against ourselves. In our power, we stay consistent with our truth and stand in the power of our truth.

To stand in our power is to be guided by truth. Life will always be consistent with how we live through our truth. In our true power, we do not go against ourselves. We know that ego strength and societal status do not represent true power. In our truth, we own our pain and heal. In our power, we radiate our truth.

CHAPTER 15

Feeling Our Pain

THE THOUGHT OF FEELING our pain can be frightening. We hold on to our fears to limit uncertainty. We keep
ourselves busy with distractions to avoid our pain. It is in
stillness that we feel with clarity. In our feelings, we see
truth. In our truth, we break through struggle and dissolve
pain and suffering. We heal when we feel our pain, face it,
and resolve it.

Feelings are the feedback we receive from the vast field
that we are a part of. To avoid our feelings is to block feeling
true freedom. We live so distracted and far away from the
truth of who we are. In our avoidance, we suffer and remain
stuck. Our feared pain becomes a barrier to our freedom.

To fear feeling our pain is to hold only what we know
as security. We live satisfied with the way things are and
control our feelings to avoid uncertainty. Our perceived
securities are emotional attachments in disguise. To feel true
security is to live from the truth of who we are. Our fears
dissolve in the light of our truth.

To avoid our pain is to constantly relive emotional pain. We live with emotional restrictions and suffer in the same challenges. We seem to repeat our perceived problems and live a life of chaos. To resolve our emotional pain, we have to feel. It is in our truth that we feel our pain and face it to end it. It is to live true to truth.

Feeling our pain needs no effort. We do not need to try to change anything to heal. Effort is an indicator that we are stuck in the division of our thoughts and truth. We observe our pain and it will dissolve through clarity of truth. We break through struggle and pain when we surrender to truth. To control our feelings is to stay stuck in a cycle of pain.

In our pain, we think we are clear in our search to feel better. We hope for happiness but are defeated by nonfulfillment. We hold on to what we think gives us security only to suffer if we lose it. We search for ways to take away our pain and get stuck in our search. We feel there is no way out of our struggle and feel trapped. It is in feeling our pain that we feel freedom.

In stillness our feelings become clear. We see and feel what has clouded our perception. Our awareness opens us to the division of our thoughts and we clearly see what has led us astray. We learn that our pain is from our misguided perception and we see what we have mistaken for truth. In stillness, we see the truth that we are and our suffering ends.

In our struggle, our feelings and emotions perpetuate struggle. We feel limited and trapped with no way out of our pain. Life adversity grows as we try to control outcomes to our satisfaction. We go against the flow of life. We go against ourselves. Breaking through struggle is to feel our pain and then end it without control.

Feeling our pain leads to freedom. Our feelings are needed feedback for our healing. Avoidance only keeps us living in fear and suffering. It is in stillness that we can feel into our pain and end our suffering. Our emotional pain dissolves in the light of our truth. We break through struggle when we are still and feel our pain.

In Our Avoidance

In silence, our feelings are loud and clear. In stillness, we cannot escape our pain. To be present with our feelings can feel raw and encompassing, so we avoid. We avoid because our pain is hard to work through. We resist because we try to hold on to feelings of familiarity. We distract ourselves to not feel. In our avoidance, we move further away from ourselves.

On our journey to find our way back to the truth of who we are, we get caught in an emotional trap. We struggle to move through our pain. We avoid discomfort and fear uncertainty. We are most often not even aware that we are avoiding emotional pain. Our body feels uncomfortable and responds with avoidance.

We avoid our feelings with constant distractions. We use drugs, alcohol, food, sugar, caffeine, watch toxic news, play games, shop, and scroll through social media to keep from being with ourselves. We are told that medications will take the pain away, only to keep the user disconnected and in a fog. It is in our avoidance that our pain remains.

Our pain does not go away when we use avoidance. To avoid is to stay stuck and not face an experience completely. Feeling our pain and avoiding are the same. We may be aware of our feelings of pain, but our entire being is also aware of the feeling of avoidance. It creates restriction in the body. We become one with what we avoid.

In our avoidance, we keep our painful memories at the surface. As long as we do not face an experience for resolution, it stays in its raw state. We continue being emotionally attached to it and we suffer. Our memories will always be there. It is our response to our memories that changes with resolution. Avoiding the uncomfortable only prolongs our suffering.

In the avoidance of our pain, we control our feelings to avoid uncertainty. We fear the feelings that we anticipate and avoid facing our pain to stay comfortable. We get stuck in the middle of our pain and feel that there is no way out. Through our control, we may avoid our feelings of pain, but we also avoid ultimate freedom.

In our avoidance, we disconnect from our true nature. We exchange peace for confinement to a life of emotional pain. We live with constant adversity. We struggle to truly connect in our relationships. We communicate superficially and avoid intimacy. To step out of avoidance, we must stand in the connection of our truth.

In our avoidance, we resist truth and what can bring us peace only to stay with what we know. We become complacent and stay stuck in struggle. We resist awareness and sabotage happiness. Life becomes a routine of adversity and emotional unrest. We wonder how to break through struggle while not realizing that we can end it right now.

In our truth, we clearly see our avoidances as a limitation to freedom. In avoidance, we suffer. To feel our pain is to leave the known and end our suffering. It is to be still, feel, and resolve our pain as we know it. In truth, we face our emotions. We live in peace and in the flow of life. It is in our truth that we feel our pain and heal.

In Stillness

In the stillness of our minds, we see clearly what we have allowed to enter. We see our painful life story up close. We see the truth about our story and it becomes clear that our thoughts have limited us from our freedom. We see that our emotional distractions kept us busy. To resolve our pain, we must be still and feel from the truth of who we are.

In stillness, we feel into the darkness of our pain. Our emotional pain meets reality. We meet our grief, depression, shame, and anger with a depth of knowing. We hear the illusive thoughts that we believed to be truth and they become silenced as false. Our painful life story transforms into a deep knowing that we are not our experiences. In stillness, we see the light.

To be still is to be in the awareness of our emotional pain without distraction. It is to see our emotional distraction as diversion from being true to ourselves. Healing begins when we intentionally go deep into the darkness of our pain, not to feel pain, but to see truth. In our truth, we are reminded of what we have forgotten: that we are always truth, as awareness.

We see truth in stillness and we transcend darkness through truth. Our suffering is consistent with our conditioning. We forget the true nature of our being and think we have to find truth. The darkness of our suffering stays alive in the not knowing of our true nature. It is in stillness that we know we are light, not the darkness of suffering.

In stillness, it is clear that our suffering is a result of a lifetime of beliefs. We know that we do not have to meet societal standards such as marital and education statuses, religious and medical standards, and the false standards of success. In stillness, we know that the truth of our being is not elevated by status.

It is in stillness that we clearly see what has been accepted as truth and we know in depth what is false. We see the thoughts that we have allowed to shape our feelings and emotions and know that our experiences are not our true nature. In stillness, we see truth come to light. We know truth in depth.

To be still is to feel truth at the depth of our being. It is to know truth deep within and feel from the truth of who we are. It is in stillness, without thought, that we see truth. We see our pain and face it to resolve it as we surrender to a deep knowing that cannot be denied. We feel into the pure essence of our being as truth.

In stillness, the pure awareness of our being shines. We see truth come to light and all suffering ends in the light of our truth. It is in our pure awareness that we see what has clouded our perception. To avoid our feelings is to allow distractions to overshadow our opening to freedom. We stay stuck in a life of suffering.

In stillness, we see our pain as a limit to our freedom. We see why our journey of healing needed to unfold and that we do not have to suffer. We see the truth of our pain and it dissolves. We override our distractions and feel free of the restrictions of our pain. To heal, we must be still and feel into truth. It is where we know freedom.

Transcending Fear through Truth

At the root of our fears there is darkness. The uncertainty of the unknown grips us at the depth of our being. Our fearful thoughts repeat. We try to fight our fears with avoidance, but they grow stronger. We think we can push through our fears with courage, only to feel powerless and withdraw. To transcend fear, we must become a light to oneself.

Our fears are deeper than we know. We think they are fleeting and are not aware of hidden emotional pain. We use superficial strength to overcome our fears, only to feel defeated in our effort. Uncertainty will tear down those who think they are strong and will shake their facades to the core. To see the root of our fears is to see them in the light of truth.

Fear has many branches. We complicate life by seeing our fears only at the surface. We fear losing what we are attached to, without knowing we are attached. We fear disease as a name, without learning about how to balance our health. We fear losing our beliefs but don't inquire about truth. To transcend fear through truth, we must inquire into the depth of fear.

In the darkness of our minds, our conditioned thoughts and beliefs keep us in a cycle of fear. The uncertainty of the unknown perpetuates dark thoughts. We believe what we think is true, so we rationalize. Our fears grow in intensity, so we numb our feelings and live confused. We distract ourselves from the truth and stay in the dark.

In our avoidance of our fears, we go against our truth. We live against the true nature of our being. Life becomes increasingly difficult when we are constantly either running or hiding from the unknown. To transcend fear, we must learn about the false in the known. It is then that we can live in truth and be the power that we are.

In our fear, we are powerless. We give our power over to alleged authority in fear of our own. We fear losing our familiar lifestyle and become satisfied with chaos. We lose ourselves in relationships in our fear of losing security. We fear death without understanding the truth of living. The lack of awareness of our fears keeps us in fear and we remain powerless.

To live in fear is to give up freedom. In fear, we block the flow of life and attach to an outcome. We fight being in peace in exchange for conflict. We limit our freedom with our fearful thoughts. In fear, our entire being is in restriction. We suffer in our fears. It is in our truth that we are free. We know we have nothing to fear in truth.

In our truth, we connect with a deep knowing that we are safe. We feel supported and completely held by the universe as a knowing of truth. We feel an immense amount of security and belonging as we surrender to the uncertainty of life. We know that all is well in the light of our truth. We feel safe as the light that we are.

In our light, we see truth. To know truth at the depth of our being is to be in peace, not fear. In truth, we face life without avoidance and trepidation. We align with the light that we are and feel held, safe, and loved. To transcend fear, we must stand in our truth and power while stepping into the unknown. It is to live as the fearless light that we are.

Breaking through Struggle

To be in struggle can feel like we are locked in with no way out. We look for methods to make our struggles go away but feel defeated in our practice. We feel powerless. We become one with struggle. We think we know the outcome of our freedom so we hold on to it tightly. We fight for our freedom but see no change. To break through struggle is to align with freedom.

In the struggles of our lives, we fight against ourselves. We avoid our feelings and get stuck in a loop of struggle. We feel trapped. The adversity in our lives grows exponentially and we think that the universe is working against us. We live against the flow of life because we think that freedom is out of reach. We become struggle.

It is in our controlled feelings and thoughts that we find struggle. There is a division between what we have been conditioned to believe and truth. We rationalize our thoughts and beliefs and attach to the names of our struggles. We suffer immensely and become one with our pain. To break through struggle is to be open to life unfolding without our control.

In our struggles, we try to control outcomes. We resist change in our hopes that life will unfold as we *think* we want. We stay stuck. The attachment to an outcome obstructs the flow of life. To break through is to align with freedom with no attachment to any specific outcome. It is in our alignment with truth that we have a breakthrough.

To live in truth is to know that we have the power to break through struggles without any external authority. It is our conditioned thoughts and beliefs that have us attaching to security from an outside source. We go against ourselves when we think that power is in those with high societal and education statuses. Truth is all we need to live the power that we seek.

Breaking through struggle is to feel our pain and end it. We transcend fear through truth and diffuse feelings of doubt in stillness. We recognize avoidance as a distraction and face our pain. We stay consistent with truth and see old thought patterns, behaviors, and unhealthy relationships as a limit to our freedom. We feel our pain, end it, and live free.

In our truth, we know that our freedom is in our power. We do not need to search for answers outside ourselves. There are no methods or steps to get us to freedom. We feel into a knowing that aligns with truth and we see truth without a fight. Our entire being must be in alignment with freedom, not attachment. It is in this alignment that we break through.

To break through, we are not giving ourselves over to a form that is higher. We are aligning our ego-self with truth as awareness. We are not connecting with awareness as if we are separate. To break through is to know in depth that our true nature is awareness. Our struggles dissolve as we surrender to the light of our truth.

In the light of our truth, we are free. We see clearly how our attachment to feelings of pain has limited our freedom and we flow with life without a fight. We know in depth that we are the power that we need. Our power is in our alignment to truth, and in our power, there is freedom. Our struggles dissolve in the knowing of the true light that we are.

CHAPTER 16

Naming Our Emotions

To put a name to our emotions brings clarity. Or does it? We identify with names as if they hold the true meaning of our existence. We hold our painful life story as the truth of who we are and struggle to move through our emotions. We become one with the names of our emotions. To heal is to remember our innate language of truth to see beyond a name for true meaning.

Naming our emotions requires us to first see how we identify with our name. We learn early in life that we are separate by name and then hold that belief. We identify with our name as who we see as our person. We see ourselves as separate from anything that is not our person. Names become everything that is filtered through the lens of separation. We *become* our name.

We name our emotions in hope of finding meaning in our life experiences. We attach to the names of our emotions and fail to face the stories of our pain. We guard our stories and hold them in defense of our pain. We see ourselves *as* our story.

To heal our emotional pain is to move beyond names and stories. It is to see that we are not our story. We are not our pain.

Naming our emotions turns into a painful reality. Names
seen through a lens of separation keep us stuck in the meaning of the name. We hold names as a justification for difficult life circumstances, without facing our pain. We stop
at the name of an emotion as if it were truth. Our reality
becomes that of duality.

To see through a clouded perception of duality limits
our healing of emotional pain. We see names as an object
or label and we are unable to integrate them into healing
for truth. We view the world from our ego identity and
remain a separate entity of thoughts misrepresenting truth.
Names are seen through a description of separation.

To live the truth of who we are is to inquire into our
innate language of truth. We are an infinite feedback of
information, and in truth, we see clearly that we are not
only names and words. We see our names and the names of
our emotions with a depth of knowing. In truth, we are able
to discern between names and the truth of knowing.

We are separate only by name. The names of our emotions separate us as being one with our pain. Naming our
emotions becomes a helpful tool to understand our emotions, but only when seen through the lens of truth. It is at
the depth of our being that we see beyond names. In truth,
we know meanings that cannot be described in words. It is
an innate knowing of truth.

To live free of names is to see the limitations in identification. It is seeing our attachment to names as security that
actually keeps us suffering. Freedom from names opens us
to becoming free of self. It is at the depth of our being that
we are able to see beyond a name for true meaning.

To be open to the truth of names gives us clarity into our dualistic mindset. We see beyond our ego identity and see the truth of who we are. We know with depth that we are not our painful life stories seen through our name. We hear and know our innate language of truth. We see past the shallow dualistic meaning of names and heal in the light of our truth.

Identified with a Name

Names capture our attention. We identify with the name that we were given at birth and only hear it as the truth of who we are. We view the world through our ego and see everything as separate. We identify others and ourselves as separate. We stop at knowing only a name. We shifted from knowing truth to only identifying with names through separation.

We are born into this world as one, but soon learn to see through a lens of division. We learn that our name is not another person or object as we see ourselves as our name. We feel divided and it shows in our actions. We treat others with disdain without remembering that we are all connected. We do not see past names as being our identity. We become one with names as that of duality.

We identify with names far deeper than we believe. We take on labels for truth, as names of emotions. We see diseases as the labels that they have been given, without understanding balanced health. We become one with labels and feel that we are the labels. It is in our awareness that we see names and labels for their false brand on our being.

We identify ourselves with the names of groups and speak of them as an added name to our existence. We emphatically identify with the names of political parties and religious groups and say that we *are* the names. We insist that we are not the names of the contrasting groups. To be identified as a name keeps division in the lead.

To stand in our true nature and connection does not imply that we must not use names. In our truth, we become free of seeing through our ego identity and name. It is about having the awareness of names while knowing truth. It is about being able to identify others by name but not feel separate. It is about living from truth.

To be identified with names is to miss out on true beauty. We see everything, including ourselves, as a name. We judge others and ourselves as being inferior to our definition of beauty. We get stuck in our ego identity and look past the beauty of nature. We and everything else are seen as words with limited meanings. Names have become a distraction to our truth.

Our identification with names has kept us distracted from seeing truth. We find meaning in names for what we believe is true and stop at knowing only what we think we know. Our curious nature has shifted to following systematic ways of being. We attach to the meaning of names and stay with the identification as being separate. We lose ourselves to names.

To come home to the true nature of our being is to know our connection beyond names. It is to open our awareness to see the limitation in identification. Names limit the way we view our connection to everything. We are separate only by name. To stand in truth is to know and feel our connection. It is to be free from our limited identity.

In the freedom from our ego and identification with names, we bring our attention to unification. We shift from division to our innate knowing of connection. We see the beauty in all, no matter the name. We clearly see the limitation of names and are open to viewing the world as unified. In our truth, we are free of ego identity. Free of names.

Our Name, Our Story

We identify with our life story through our name. We live attached to our past traumas and struggles and defend our pain as a result of our story. We struggle to see past our name that holds the painful events of our lives. We share our story only for others to see us *as* our story. We lose ourselves to our story and *become* our story. We see ourselves as *our* name, *our* pain, and *our* story.

We all have a life story. It is the emotional attachment to the pain of our story that keeps us in suffering. We attach to the familiar feelings of a false sense of safety and rationalize our position. We identify with our life story through our name and fail to see the connection to our struggles. We stay emotionally attached to our pain.

Our names and stories hold significant weight in our beliefs about ourselves. Names are blamed for labeling ill luck, while our life story can shame us into depression for a lifetime. We are so attached to our names and stories that we feel that if we change our name or move our location that our emotional pain will all go away. In our truth, we can see the falsity in our beliefs.

In truth, we know that our name and story cannot be changed for expected power. We know that we cannot change our story by harnessing power from names of deities from ancient past. We know that our power does not lie in the ego identity of another. In our truth, we know that we are already the true power that we seek.

Our struggle to see past our name keeps us in a loop of struggle and pain. To hold a limited view of being only our name and story has us projecting our misguided perception onto others to see them only for their names and stories. We stay stuck in a loop of sharing our pain and seeing each other only for names and stories. We distract ourselves from truth.

We hold on to our life story and say it is a part of who we are. We add on new stories without facing our previous pain. We keep health labels as if they were our new name. We justify our struggles as an inevitable result of our traumas and accept a slim chance of resolution. We live through our stories.

The memories of our painful life stories haunt us. We keep the names of our traumatic events alive, whether we share or avoid them. It is in our truth that we know we cannot hide from our pain. Our memories will always remain, but our emotional pain dissolves in truth. It is in truth that we break the cycle of pain seen through our name and story.

To heal our pain is to open our hearts to the knowing of truth. Our identification with our names and stories keeps us separate and in pain. It is in our truth that we know that we are only separate by name and story. In truth, we feel unified as the pure awareness that we are. We feel free of our pain, our names, and our stories.

Identifying with our life story through our name keeps us in suffering. In our truth, we see beyond stories and names. We feel a deep inner knowing that we are not our story. We are not our pain seen through our name. In truth, we open our hearts to seeing others and ourselves as the truth of who we are. It is in our truth that we are not limited to our names and stories.

Our Innate Language

Naming our emotions brings understanding to our feelings. We learn to identify our emotions to understand pain and heal. It is our misguided understanding of names and words that keeps us attached to our pain. As we open to truth, we connect with a language that goes beyond names, beyond words. We remember what we have forgotten: our *innate* language.

To remember our innate language is to know instantly what is true or false. We get stuck in the meaning of words and it clouds our perception. Healing can take a lifetime when we attach to words that defy the truth of who we are. We are able to see the false meaning of words when they are filtered through the knowing of our innate universal language.

We are all in constant exchange with a vast flow of memory as information. Every thought generated remains as universal memory. We have access to every thought transmitted through space and time. To know this gives us an immense responsibility to be aware of our words and actions. We are all individual minds connected as one conscious mind.

Our true innate language is love with no hate or divisiveness. Our thinking becomes muddied by our conditioned beliefs. We get caught in a loop of distorted thoughts and receive back what we send out. We find ourselves further from the language that is inherent in all of us. We block the flow of our innate language and stay in the confinement of dualistic thinking.

To remain open to our innate language is to be in truth. In our truth, we connect with a language that goes beyond names and words. There is a deep inner knowing that cannot be described. We question only the false because we know truth in depth. In our truth, we come back to the language that is innate in all of us.

We are born into this world only knowing our innate language. We easily absorb different languages without any effort. We are one with all information and live in the flow. It is only as we grow older that we gradually move out of our natural flow. In our awareness, we break the cycle. We remember a deep knowing.

It is our misguided understanding of names and words that limits our life progress. We struggle in our daily lives without being aware that information is available to us. We only know what we know until we expand our awareness. It is in our awareness that we see beyond names and words and become aware of the flow of true information.

Our innate language is not something we have to learn. It is inherent in all of us. We do not have to connect to it as if we were separate. We are one with it, taking on a different frequency and form. We are always connected. Seeing through the lens of our ego will keep us thinking that we are separate. Our connection is in our knowing.

To be in the flow of our innate language is to get out of our own way. We stay open and we see the cycle of dualistic thinking. We feel instant understanding and knowing of our feelings and emotions while our attachment to our pain dissolves. We remember and know our *true* language at the depth of our being. It is a language of love and unity.

Free of Names

At the depth of our being there is truth. In truth, we know more than our name. We know that we are not our painful life story as seen through our name. We see the limitation in our identification with names and end the attachment to our pain. We name our pain, but only through the lens of truth. It is in our truth that we become free of self as seen through a name.

To be free of names is to really know why we find so much security in a name. We find security in what gives our ego-character security. We hold our emotional pain through our name and attach to what we *think* is giving us security. We see through a misguided perception of seeing security through our ego as our name. In our false security, we stay restricted.

Freedom from names is to live without attachments. We see certainty within names and hold on to our beliefs. We attach to names as credentials and accolades and think that they will earn us a higher place in society. We stay confined to our attachments and beliefs and navigate through life as the names we think we are. Who would we be if we were free of names?

We are conditioned to believe that we are separate by name. We take on a mechanistic view of separation that is supported as the "correct" scientific model. We are shut down as quacks, charlatans, heretics, and minority fringe if we question our true nature. The question is, are we willing to come home to our truth and see beyond names and beyond separation?

To be free of names is to not stand divided as a name. Our division shows through the illusion of belonging to the name of a political party, country, spiritual group, or religion. In our truth, we become aware that we belong everywhere and are a part of everything. In our freedom, we live free of names and borders. We live unified as one.

In our truth, we connect with more than a name. We connect with all memory as information. We have access to all memory that goes beyond words and names. Our suffering is in the names that we use and we can end it right now. To live in our truth is to know that we are free of the limits of names.

In our freedom from names, we see the limitation in identification. We clearly see names and labels as limited in meaning. We see the pain from our life story as an emotional attachment and we end our attachment. We use names as a tool, but not as the true meaning of our existence. It is in the freedom of names that we see beyond our limits in identification.

Living free of self, as seen through a name, is to live in awareness. Our ego identity gets in the way and needs our attention. We sleepwalk through life as a name. We further name our pain, only to become our pain. We are not our pain or stories seen through a name. We are beings of truth that are as free as the light that we are.

In our truth, we know more than a name. We remember what we have forgotten. In the knowing of the truth of our being, we know in depth what is beyond our ego identity, and we see truth from falsity. We know the true meaning of names as filtered through truth. It is at the depth of our being that we are free of names.

CHAPTER 17

Expressing Our Pain

WE EXPRESS OUR EMOTIONAL pain through the illusion of our ego. We see and feel our existence as our ego identity and express ourselves from a conditioned mindset. Healing our emotional pain is to see our ego-self from the pure essence of our being. We are then able to express ourselves as balanced and know who is expressing emotional pain.

Our existence and expressions through our ego are very real. We need our body and ego to navigate through life, but we get caught in the belief that we are only our physical body and mind. In the belief that our ego-character is the truth of who we are, we mislead ourselves. We are illuminated by one light that is true awareness.

Our emotional experiences are expressed through our ego. We identify with the material world and seek power, money, material possessions, and societal recognition. We express ourselves from what we have or have not, as truth to our worth. There is a misconception in our belief that something outside of us will elevate who we are.

We live through our pain and express ourselves as pain. We see our emotional pain expressed as struggle in our lives because we see and feel our existence as our accumulated experiences. We forget truth and see our unresolved memories come through our expressions. We live in struggle and against the flow of life.

In our emotional pain, we express ourselves through constant doing. We distract ourselves from opening up by avoiding uncomfortable feelings. We use technology, drugs, food, work, and relationships to keep us busy. We fight for peace through protests and war, while not realizing that the fight is literally against ourselves. It is in our awareness that we live in peace.

In our emotional pain, we take our feelings out on others and ourselves. Our emotional pain is expressed as chaos in our lives as we attach to people, places, things, events, and beliefs. We act as if the world is working against us when our struggles are showing us that we are working against ourselves. It is in our truth that we express ourselves as truth.

To express from truth is to open to our true nature as awareness. We attach to who we believe we are and assign our worth based on that illusion. Our expression of who we *think* we are becomes a false narrative of our appearances, names, and credentials. In awareness, we express ourselves through the knowing of our truth.

In our attention to truth, we see who we truly are. We observe our conditioned ego-self from the pure essence of our being and instantly see the illusion. We transcend the duality of our ego-structures and live in the light of our truth. It is in the observation of the ego that we live aware through life and express ourselves as a balanced being.

We heal emotional pain when our ego-structures are overcome. We transcend our duality mindset and see beyond our ego identity. Our conditioned identity is seen through the truth of who we are and dissolves in the light of truth. We express ourselves from a balanced ego and we integrate our knowing into our lives. We identify with our true nature, not an illusion.

The Illusion of Self

We identify with an illusory existence. We express ourselves through who we think we are without knowing or questioning truth. We identify only as our ego-character, without understanding it is a mask to our truth. We feel trapped in our struggles and think that freedom is not available to us. Our freedom is in the knowing of the illusion of the ego.

We identify with our limited self-structures as the truth of who we are. We see our physical body and appearance as truth and express ourselves through that illusion. We build a character that we believe will add value to who we are by using clothes, cosmetics, tattoos, and jewelry. We have lost our knowing of truth and hold on to an illusion.

As the illusion of the self, we go along with what we are told without question. We get trapped in the interference of religions, governments, and school systems and take the messages and teachings as truth. We are unaware that our awareness is a threat to the power structures of the world. To give our power over is to lose to the illusion. We *become* the illusion.

In the illusion, we think we must believe what others tell us is truth. We fail to see a controlled narrative and follow along without question. We limit our freedom and sovereignty, only seeing our existence through our ego identity. In our personal inquiry, we break free of controlled narratives. We see truth.

As the illusion of the self, we chase spiritual awareness through the teachings of others. We interpret life from a perception that is based on a false sense of self and express spiritual discoveries through that illusion. People express themselves as enlightened when life is still seen through a lens of duality. It is in our personal awareness and discernment that we see truth.

In the illusion of self, we stay restricted, confused, and powerless. We lack clear direction and search for guidance and rescue. We become complacent with the familiar and suffer in our struggles. We either try to control outcomes or wait for something outside of us to change. Our freedom is in our clarity and power and in the freedom of our truth.

To view life through the illusion of the ego is to get trapped in illusory struggles. We struggle in our personal, social, and work lives. We see our struggles with health, finances, and daily problems as inevitable parts of life. We feel locked in and see ourselves as our struggles. Our freedom from struggle is in the knowing of our true nature.

Our ego identity is needed to navigate through life. It is in the illusion of self that we sleepwalk through life. In our awareness, we live with a balanced ego while knowing our truth. We see problems as an illusion and feel free. We inquire into personal truth and find our own answers. In awareness, we know truth.

In the knowing of our truth, our ego identity as we know it dissolves. We live through a balanced ego. We find meaning in our existence and use curiosity to view the world as an appearance. We expand our awareness and see beyond our known perception. We awaken to what has always been available to us. We know who we truly are.

Attention to Truth

Is the expression of who we are who we see in the mirror? We express ourselves through our emotions, behaviors, and actions, but who is expressing? We have forgotten our true nature and only identify as our physical form. In our journey back to remembering our truth, we learn from our greatest teacher: the ego. To live our truth, we must give attention to truth.

To be a witness to the expression of the character that we identify with as the ego unites us with the knowing of the true essence of our being. We construct our entire life around holding self-structures that we believe will keep us safe, yet we feel confined to limitations. We feel fear in the uncertainty of dissolving structured beliefs while unaware it is where our freedom lies.

Our search for our truth is most often pursued through meditation, but there is no structured spiritual or religious path and no methods that can guarantee truth. We come home to ourselves through being grounded in our awareness and observing truth. It is in the absence of our ego that we remember what has been forgotten.

Observing our ego sheds light on our emotional attachments. We clearly see that our true nature is not who is attached. Our attention shows us that it is our ego-character that is attached to our emotions and beliefs. Emotional attachments to people, places, things, and beliefs dissolve in the light of our attention from the knowing of the pure essence of our being.

To observe the conditioned self from pure awareness is to feel a deep knowing that cannot be conceptualized. It is an innate knowing that is free of learned thoughts and beliefs. It is free of thought, but alive as truth. It is in this pure awareness that we dissolve the ego-structures that keep us tied to a life of suffering.

To see non-separation is to be free of the duality of thoughts and beliefs. It is to be aware of the pure awareness that we are. It is in an instantaneous flash of knowing, where we are seeing from beyond our ego-character. We see everything just as is. There is no thought, because where there is thought, there is separation through a perception of conditioned beliefs.

To be attentive as the truth of who we are, we understand the role of our ego-self is to navigate through this life, which allows us to learn through experiences. We must not hate the ego, because it is a great teacher. We need our ego to show us what we need for healing. As we expand our awareness, we feel gratitude for insight that we see through our attention.

We will always have an ego as long as we are living as a human. It is our self-structures and emotional attachments that hold us in restriction. To be free of self-structures is to see them through the pure essence of our awareness. It is in the clarity of our truth that our ego-structures as we know them dissolve. We see the illusion in what we considered truth.

To see through the power of attention is to see truth. We see that we are not only our physical form. We feel free of the limitations that are held through our ego. Our emotional pain as attachment dissolves in the light of our observation and we feel in peace. We live and express ourselves as a balanced being. We live true to our true awareness.

Balanced Expression

How can we be completely attentive to the expression of our ego-character to be in alignment with the truth of who we are? In our unawareness, our distractions and routines pull us away from our truth as we align with attachment and avoidance. We easily default to our past conditioning and live in conflict. In awareness, we live and express balance.

To observe our expressions in our everyday lives allows us to be aware of our behavior, while still knowing the pure awareness of our being. It is to allow life to flow as it comes and to transition into the next moment without resistance. Being aware of how we express ourselves helps bring us into balance as we use our words, thoughts, and wisdom to align with our actions and behaviors.

To express ourselves through the ego without awareness has us doing what keeps us in suffering. We express ourselves through our pain as we hold expectations and attach to desired outcomes. We use distractions and avoidance to numb our discomfort while we get stuck in emotional patterns. We stay locked in behaviors that defy our truth.

In our unawareness, we express ourselves through our ego with conflict. We argue instead of making peace. We use words that hurt others and ourselves. We live with shame and regret, without seeing resolution. In unawareness, our lives are burdened with struggles and emotional pain. We see no way out of struggle. Our freedom is in our awareness.

A balanced expression is to be aware of our behavior while still knowing our truth. We listen to the words that we speak and see our behaviors as they are expressed. We recognize dualistic thinking and end it. Breaking free of our conditioned structures requires attention. It is in our awareness that we stay in alignment with truth.

To be aware of our expressions is to see what aligns with truth. We see that life is mirroring back to us the frequency that we are. We observe external annoyances for what needs to be transformed from within. We recognize hate, violence, and divisiveness as being expressed through a dualistic mindset. We live through our truth. We live awake.

To express ourselves through balance is to live in balance. We live in the flow of life and feel peace. It is to stay focused and aware of our responses and behaviors. We are kind to others and ourselves. We make decisions that align with truth and we do not go against ourselves. Our balanced expression radiates into our surroundings and beyond.

To express ourselves as a balanced being is a contribution to a healthy collective mindset. We share the memory of our being with the collective memory. Our thoughts, behaviors, and expressions matter to share peace, not pain. It is a great responsibility to know this as truth. We see balance in our personal lives as confirmation we are making a difference.

Our balanced expressions are indicative of our focused awareness. In our awareness we see clearly, and therefore express ourselves with clarity. We see intended distractions and avoidances and come back into focus. We stay attentive to truth and live free of conflict. Our ego-structures dissolve in our awareness as we do our best to express truth and live free of duality.

Transcending Duality

We view the world through a dualistic lens. We express our thoughts through our ego-character as "me versus other" or "this versus that." We use judgment to conclude what we believe is right or wrong or good or bad. It is in our surrender to the uncertainty of truth that we live truth. It is where we feel freedom from opposition and transcend the duality of our mind.

To see through our ego-structures is to see through a dualistic lens. Through our ego, we see everyone and thing as separate. It is in our awareness that we can use our ego to navigate through life while knowing the true nature of our being. It is in our conditioned ways that we go against our truth and live in duality. In our awareness, we transcend duality.

In our emotional pain, we are caught in the dualistic illusion of the ego. We see everything we think is not working in our favor as working against us. We fight against the flow of life only to create more problems. We live in conflict with others and ourselves. In the duality of the mind, we live restricted. To transcend duality is to see truth.

In duality, we live in contradiction to our truth. We search for belonging without remembering it is not outside of us. We struggle to see past our conditioning and think that names, degrees, and societal recognition will ensure a safe place of belonging. It is in the ending of our attachment to false beliefs that we feel a deep knowing that we belong. We feel truth.

In a dualistic mindset, we judge. We see others and ourselves as right or wrong. We compete and knock others down to look better. We mistake greed for success and see those with more as successful. It is in our freedom from duality that we see that we are all one conscious mind. The success of one is the success of all. To judge one is to judge all.

In duality, we are incredibly selfish. We cannot see past our emotional pain and problems. We stay focused on our problems without knowing that we each contribute our thoughts and experiences to the collective memory. It is in our awareness that we contribute with an open heart. We live as the love that we all are.

In the transcendence of duality, our minds align with the universe as one. We feel completely open with genuine love and compassion for all existence. Our ego-structures as we know them dissolve. Our fear of uncertainty dissolves in the light of our truth and we surrender to a deep knowing. We remember the truth of who we are.

In our remembrance, we feel free of attachments to outcomes. We recognize synchronicities that are too profound to ignore and understand that our experience is needed for our evolution. It becomes a mission to share our truth with the collective. We feel as if the universe steps in to help in any way needed. We live in the flow of life. We live in peace.

To transcend the duality of the mind is to live in the light of our truth. We see through truth and continue to break down ego-structures. We stay united with the transcendent and know that the ego is not the pure essence of our being. It is in this knowing that we express our emotions as balanced. It is in the transcendence of duality that we are free.

CHAPTER 18

Facing Our Pain

WE ARE FACED WITH truth in the absence of avoidance. Our emotional pain is clear, but in this moment of clarity, we face truth to heal. We end our attachment to the known and our suffering ends. In times of distraction, we use our awareness to come back to being present. Facing our pain leads us to peace. To be free, we must face our pain.

Facing our pain is to be present as the light beings that we are. In our light, we feel no fear. We feel safe in our being and open to our light. In our pain, we feel restricted and we suffer. To see our pain for truth is to be present and feel. It becomes clear that we are not our pain, but pure awareness as a witness. In the light of truth, our pain dissolves.

Facing our pain is not to move through our emotions. Moving through our pain takes time and effort. To face our pain is to be present without thought or revisiting trauma. In our presence, truth is seen and pain dissolves. To try and move through our pain is to get stuck in the middle and to regress into further restriction. To be free of pain is to face it and end it.

In the avoidance of our pain, we distract. Our body feels uncomfortable and our attention is diverted to a distraction. We numb our pain in clever ways of our individual choice while staying stuck in our suffering. It is in the facing of our pain that we see instant relief. We are faced with truth in the absence of distraction. Our pain dissolves in our truth.

To face our pain is to see the truth of resistance. We stay in resistance in both our attachment to and our avoidance of emotional pain. Facing our pain is to completely be with our pain. We see it, feel it, and end it. It is in our awareness that we see resistance as a fight against ourselves. It is in facing our pain that our suffering ends. We are open to seeing truth.

In the presence of our emotional pain, our justifications for our suffering come to an end. We see the struggles that were once seen as inevitable due to our past as emotional attachments. It is in our attachment to the known that we stay with the known. To heal is to face our pain and end all emotional attachments.

Facing our pain leads to peace. To live in peace does not require us to fight for peace. We live in peace without conflict and suffering because peace is the true nature of our being. If we are not in peace, we are in struggle. It is in the facing of our pain that our suffering dissolves and we feel deep inner peace as freedom.

In the freedom of pain, our entire being feels free. We feel open to the light that we are with an abundant sense of safety and belonging. Facing our pain allows us to come back to the truth of who we are. In our pain, we stay in restriction. In our freedom, we feel open and one with the universe. To be free we must face our pain.

In the freedom from pain, we live free and in peace. We open to the light that we are and heal our emotional pain instantly. We see our suffering end in the ending of our emotional attachments. We live aware of distractions and come back to the present to face our pain. We live in the light of our truth and face the truth of our pain.

Facing Truth in Pain

Emotional pain grips us at the depth of our being. We fear the unknown, so we attempt to hide. We avoid our feelings and distract ourselves. We hold the familiar as security, only to stay attached to the known. It is in truth that we see into our pain for it to lead us to freedom. To be free of our pain, we must face the truth of our pain.

To face our feelings, emotions, and experiences is to see them as fact. We see them with the attention of our entire being. We can clearly see that we are frightened of facing our pain because it leads to an ending of what we are holding as security. Our false securities keep us attached to the known. To see the truth of our pain brings the false to light.

In truth, we face our emotions without fear. There is no fear in truth. We know that we are safe in our connection as one with the universe. We see the truth of our fear and it dissolves into light. It is in this knowing that we surrender to truth and live in the light of our truth. We instantly see that facing the truth of our pain is to be free.

Distracting ourselves from facing our pain keeps us in resistance. Avoiding our feelings has them growing in intensity. Our being feels the suppression of memories and the emotions that we hide. There is intelligence in our existence that cannot be manipulated with avoidance. We heal when we face the truth of our pain.

In our emotional pain, we find security in familiarity. We feel safer in the known, so we stay with what we know. Our avoidance in facing our pain keeps us in suffering. We get stuck. We wonder why our lives are so difficult, but we rationalize our position. Could life be as easy as stepping out of the known and facing the truth of our pain?

We think we face our pain when we acknowledge that we have a problem. We see fault, but we never ask deep questions as to why the problem exists. It is accepted as a surface level issue without seeing the deeper emotional pain. We see the hidden pain when we face it with our complete attention. Our pain dissolves when we face it in the light of our truth.

To face our pain is to be with our feelings. We remain with them with undivided attention until truth is clear. Our emotional pain is very real and can feel incredibly raw. To avoid it is to prolong our pain and suffering. We face and feel our pain to end it. In our pain, our entire being stays in resistance. In the light of our truth, our pain dissolves.

To see our pain in the light of truth opens us to peace. In truth, we are shown peace. Facing our emotions brings clarity. We see clearly that our pain is in our emotional attachment to our suffering, and we unequivocally stand with peace. It is in facing our emotions that we see our pain cannot stand up to peace. We choose the peace that we are.

Facing the truth of our pain leads to freedom. We see the false security in the pain that we hold, so we do not avoid. We stay with our pain until we end our emotional attachment. Our emotional pain turns to peace in the instant that we face it with complete attention. We see our suffering for what it is. To be free of our pain, we must face the truth of our pain and end it.

Ending Emotional Attachments

The thought of ending an attachment is frightening. We hold on so tightly to people, places, things, events, traditions, and beliefs in an attempt to attain a sense of security. We attach to what we *think* we love only to be devastated if we lose it. In our attachment to life, we fear death, not grasping the depth of living. Ending emotional attachments leads to freedom.

We attach to what or whom we feel can provide us with a sense of security. We think we know what will bring us security as we hold desires and try to control outcomes. It is through our limited, conditioned thoughts and beliefs that we see a false security as truth. Our security in our emotional attachments proves to be hollow in meaning in the light of truth.

We attach to relationships, groups, political, and religious affiliations, as well as financial, education, and social statuses in our hope for security and belonging. These attachments are based on division because they are seen through our conditioned beliefs. It is in our attachments that we feel alone, confused, and out of place. We feel true connection when emotional attachments end.

In our attachments, we see love as security. We attach to what we believe we love and try to secure our comfort in the known. To feel true love is to strip all attachments away and stand sober in the light of our truth. In truth, we see what is false. It is only then that we can truly see the difference between love and attachment. There is no fear in losing love when we are in truth.

Our fears are deceptive when they come through as attachments. We fear losing what we assign meaning. We fear endings when it is our attachments that we fear losing. We fear death as we attach to our failures, regrets, health, money, and future hopes. It is through living without attachments that we can truly live.

Freedom from our attachments does not mean being free of one thing only to cling to another. Freedom is not limited to the actuality of confinement or the limitations of thought. It is to flow with life, no matter the circumstance. It is to live completely unrestricted from emotional attachments. Freedom begins when emotional attachments end.

To face our pain is to see our emotional attachments as the pain of our life story. We find a false sense of security in our pain. Our pain feels familiar and we hold it with conviction. We get stuck in the pain of our story and suffer. To end our suffering is to end our emotional attachment to the pain of our life story. We face our pain and end it to feel free.

Freedom from attachments is feeling completely free of restrictions. It is to end emotional attachments, without a feeling of lacking anything. It is to stand completely in peace in our universal connection. Freedom from emotional attachments is to stand alone, without feeling lonely. It is to feel completely free.

We are free of pain when we are free of emotional attachments. We feel a genuine sense of security in our connection beyond our attachments. The love we feel is infinite without measure. We do not fear endings because our emotional attachments dissolve in the light of our truth. We truly grasp the depth of living and feel free without suffering. We flow with life.

The Absence of Distraction

In the avoidance of facing our emotional pain, we stay stuck in our suffering. We distract ourselves from all feelings leading to freedom and peace. The knowing of our true nature is pushed aside as we continue to numb our pain. In our awareness, we catch our behavior in its tracks and we come back to peace. It is in the absence of distraction that we are free.

Freedom from suffering is right at that junction of feeling and distracting. We get tricked into our feelings of familiar comfort that have us following through to the behaviors we use to distract. Freedom comes when we catch ourselves in the act and come back to truth. It is in this feeling that we feel the absence of separation. We feel at home in the peace of our being.

We are faced with truth in the absence of distraction. We know in depth that the feeling that we are seeking through a distraction is already within. In our truth, we feel the true nature of our being as peace. Our reliance upon a person, object, or experience to fill us with a sense of peace ends. We know our freedom is in the truth of our being.

In the absence of distraction we are not drugged and in a fog. There is clarity where there was confusion. The alcohol, drugs, and medications distracting us from our feelings are seen as barriers to being in true peace. It is in our avoidance that we are staying in the suffering of our fragmented memory. In our clarity, we choose to be in the peace of balanced memory.

To know our true nature in depth is to embrace truth. We see distractions as moving us further away from our truth and we find no interest in a false sense of security. Our freedom is instantly cut off as soon as we use distractions. In the depth of knowing the peace of our being, we stay with true freedom as peace. Instead of distracting to move away, we move closer to truth.

In the absence of distraction, we live in the present. We are not stuck in the frequency of the past or searching for a solution in the future. All we need is in knowing the stillness of our being. All searching comes to an end in the facing of our suffering and we live as peace. We shine as we are illuminated by the light that we are.

In facing our pain our resistance dissolves. We remain completely engaged in the moment and grounded in calm. Any restriction in our being tells us that we are back to a past frequency of pain, so we end it. We know in depth that once we recognize the true nature of our being, there is no person, object, or experience that can replace the freedom that we feel.

Distraction wanes in our freedom. We continue to strengthen our resolve in presence. We live true to all feelings leading to peace and freedom. The facing of our pain has shown the false sense of security that it holds and we stand with true freedom. We see distractions as they come and we come back to truth. We live true to our true peace and freedom.

In the absence of avoiding our emotional pain, we feel peace. We face our pain and we feel into the peace that we are. The knowing of our true nature has us choosing truth, not pain. We feel no reason to distract. In our awareness, we live in our truth. It is in the absence of distraction we know in depth that we are peace, so we look no further.

In Peace

Is it humanly possible to be in peace? Peace seems to be so far away for most people. We adapt to conflict and respond to others with unkind words and actions. We get hurt and close our hearts. We clutter our minds and spaces. We shame others and ourselves. We resist peace by attaching to struggle. To be in peace is to end all attachments to conflict and *be* peace.

We live in a world with extreme conflict and divisiveness. There is ongoing fighting, protests, and war. We believe we are fighting for peace by opposing injustice, but it keeps us divided, standing against the other. To live in personal conflict proves to be a microcosm of our never-ending wars. We say we want peace, but our actions show differently.

To be in peace is to completely end our attachments to what does not live in the light of our truth. Peace does not mean to be in meditation all the time. In peace, we live a life that flows. Our responses to heightened emotional moments remain calm. We navigate through life without struggle. Life is effortless when we are in peace.

We put in great effort to hold on to our visions and thoughts of peace. We try hard to reach goals and think relationships, money, power, and societal success will bring us peace, but we are only left feeling empty. We attach to what we believe will give us peace. In our effort to find peace we move further away from it.

Peace is not found outside of ourselves. Our hope for peace and response to the world around us begins within. No one can give us peace, nor can it be taken away. No person, thing, or physical place will give us complete safety and belonging to feel in peace. Peace is not found in people, things, money, or power. It is our responsibility to be in peace. To be in peace, we must *be* peace.

To be in peace is to live peace through truth. All attachments, motives, greed, and fear in uncertainty lead to suffering. We feel pain when we fill our minds with words that we hold as truth. We see our pain reflected in our surroundings and relationships. In our pain, we close our hearts and live true to suffering. To be in peace is to live unrestricted with open hearts to truth.

Peace is love that is extended outward. We extend out what we feel within. We are one with the universe and the universe is one with us. As we open our hearts and extend love and gratitude, we feel filled with peace, love, and gratitude. It is in our shared awareness that we feel completely safe, held, loved, and in peace.

To be in peace is to know it is our true nature. Peace is not something that is attained from a reached expectation or desire. We do not find true peace in people or material possessions. Peace is always available to us. To be in peace is to come back to our truth. It is to live through the light that we are.

To be in peace is to be a light to oneself. When we shine our light, we are a light to the entire universe. We feel an abundant sense of love, comfort, and safety that fills us with peace. It is beyond what is imagined in the attachment to a desired hope. There is freedom in knowing that, yes, we can face our pain and be in peace.

CHAPTER 19

Resonance Transformation

WE ARE HAUNTED BY painful memories of the past. Our response to the painful events of our lives leaves a fragmented resonance. Our unresolved emotional pain has us repeating patterns as we attract similar resonant experiences. In our pain, we live out of resonance with our truth. To heal, we must transform our resonant memory.

The resonance of our memory shows through the expression of our being. Patterns of memory connected through time hold a frequency of harmony or dissonance. We express ourselves through our behavior, health, and relationships from our resonant frequency. It is in our expressions that we see balance or imbalance.

Emotional events in our lives affect the resonant frequency of our being. Our unresolved emotional pain fragments our resonance. We see the dissonance come through our life struggles. We repeat patterns and get stuck in a loop of pain and struggle. To transform our resonance, we must heal our emotional pain.

In our pain, we attract similar experiences as the past. We live through the frequency that we are and feel an attraction to similar frequencies. We feel strong bonds to present relationships that are similar to past experiences. We repeat patterns similar to our parents' or other significant figures'. To break the cycle is to heal the fragmented patterns of our resonant memory.

To transform our resonance to heal is to end emotional attachments. We face the pain of the painful events of our lives and end our attachment to our suffering. We do not go back and change the event through visualization. The event remains a fact. It is in our attachment that we suffer. To end an emotional attachment is to completely align with our intention and end it.

Transforming our resonance is to be in alignment with truth. In our pain there is disorder. In our truth there is order. To be in resonance with truth is to come into resonance with universal order. We align with this energy in its natural frequency that we share. We do not suffer when we are in alignment with truth.

To transform our resonance is to extend healing to the entire collective. We heal patterns of pain that have been there for generations. Healing pain from the past is extended to future generations. We are individual minds connected as one conscious mind. The transformation of one is healing for all. We are all one—everyone.

To transform emotional memory is to be free. We feel free of pain and suffering. We know we are healed of our emotional pain when we are not rattled by the memories of the past. Our resonant memory of past events is right here in the present. We heal when we face our pain now and end our attachment. In our transformation there is freedom. In freedom there is peace.

To transform our resonance is to no longer be troubled with painful memories of the past. Our emotions, behaviors, health, and relationships show as resonance in harmony. Balanced emotional memory equals balanced resonance. We live a life of balanced flow and evolve in alignment with truth. In our transformation, we heal emotional memory and live as truth.

Resonant Memory

We connect with our past through our memories. Our entire being transmits and receives information as memory. We connect with memories through similarity as we align with another resonant frequency. It is the frequency of our emotions that has us remembering our memories or those of the collective. We are one with *all* memory.

We connect with memories in alignment with the frequency of emotions. We ignite memories of the past as we align with that frequency. In our painful memories, there is attachment. In our attachment, there is fragmented resonance in a holding pattern. To heal is to transform the resonance of our emotional memory.

Patterns of memory hold a frequency of harmony or discord and we are an expression of it. We transmit and receive information that reflects the frequency that we are. We see reflections of frequency in our emotions, health, relationships, and life circumstances. In our awareness, we see where there is balance or imbalance. We see truth in patterns of memory.

We connect with memories in our alignment with similar frequencies. A memory that comes in a flash can be mistaken as a memory from a past life. Our memories may be those of another. We feel a strong connection to a memory from the alignment of resonant frequency. We are all connected and share all memory of the collective. Our memories show our connection.

We see our personal memories as we align with past frequencies we may have forgotten. We act out similar behaviors as our parents or other significant figures when our being remembers what we may avoid to forget. Our emotional memories are indicators of the resonant frequency that we are. We see our resonance through our emotions and behaviors.

The fragmented resonant memory of our being shows through our distractions, habits, addictions, and relationships. Our hidden emotional pain reverberates through life as we repeat patterns that resonate at the same frequency of previous experiences. We feel secure with familiarity and get stuck in similar patterns. Our painful memories show through our life experiences.

We hold onto our most painful memories. We see past traumas replay in our minds as we become one with our stories. Our past traumas become similar repeated traumas of the present as we resonate with the emotions of our past experiences. It is in our awareness that we face our pain and end our emotional attachment to our suffering.

The transformation to a balanced resonant memory resonates as peace. Emotional memories of the past come up and then fade away without a heightened emotional response. We do not judge others or ourselves for our past. We live in balanced flow with life without struggle. Our resonance echoes as balance into the collective. Our peace is peace for all.

We transform our resonant memory through our emotions. We face our pain right here in the present. We see our pain for the frequency that we are in this moment. We transform our emotional memories by transforming the resonance of our being through our emotions. In our transformation, our resonant memory resonates as balance and peace.

Fragmented Resonance

Can an individual be completely whole? We see through a dualistic perception. We show our internal division as we fight and compete against others. We live in fear and avoidance and hold onto our pain. Our lives mirror the fragmentation of our being. In our division, we live out of alignment with universal order. We live fragmented.

To be whole is to be in complete balance. It is to see order in all areas of our lives. It is too common to see balance in one area and have complete disorder in another. We are fragmented beings, and it shows through our fragmented lives. In our awareness, we see where we need to bring order to disorder.

Fragmented resonance is reflected in our lives as struggle. Our pain is held in a resonant holding pattern as we resist the flow of life. We hold on and try to control outcomes. In balanced resonance, we do not fear or avoid change. We live in the flow of life. In our struggle, we remain scattered in thought and fight against ourselves.

Our fight within is extended out to others. Our fragmented resonance shows as division as we stand separate in our views. We compete for who is better and fight for who is right or wrong. We remain divided. We live in rivalry with others without seeing we are fighting against ourselves. In our division, we fail to see our connection. We fail to see the division within.

In our fragmented resonance, we block the flow with our universal field of memory as information. We live inconsistently with universal order and become one with disorder. Our exchange of information becomes corrupted as we convey conflict and expect peace in return. It is in our awareness that we know that we receive back the frequency that we are.

We resonate with similar frequencies. Our fragmented resonant frequency shows through our relationships and the way we live. We blame others for our troubles without inquiring within. We find familiar comfort in believing that our pain is an inevitable result of our past. To see disorder around us reflects the fragmentation of our being. Our peace is in knowing that our conflicts are ours to resolve.

We keep generations of pain alive as we hold on to fragmented patterns of resonance. We live in the present through past experiences. We align with the frequency of the past and *become* the past. It is our responsibility to heal in this present moment. Our pain and conflict are ours to heal. Our resonance reverberates throughout the collective and into future generations.

To heal fragmented resonant patterns is to bring balance to fragmentation. We heal the areas of our lives where we see disorder. We inquire within for answers and discern for ourselves what is true or false. We lead healthy lives and bring balance to imbalance. We stand in the awareness of our connection with the universe and transfer love and light.

Our transformation from fragmented beings to balanced beings brings peace. We feel our universal connection and stand united as one. We transcend fear through truth and move through our emotional pain. We see a life of balance that reflects our transformed resonance. We are in peace as we live in alignment with universal order. In our peace, we feel whole.

Resonance of Truth

To resonate as truth is to *live* truth. Truth is recognizing the resonation with fragmentation as a false sense of security. It is to be free of emotional pain, struggle, and the limitation of control. To resonate as truth is to feel a deep sense of safety and belonging. In truth, we feel supported by the universe because we are in alignment with our true nature. Resonance of truth is to live true to truth.

The resonance of truth implies order. In our emotional pain and struggle, we fragment our resonance and live in disorder. We become complacent with familiarity as security and try to control outcomes to stay comfortable. In our disordered lives, we suffer with conflict and struggle. In truth, we resonate as balance and peace.

To resonate with truth is to stand true to the truth of who we are. We live aware at all times to not go against ourselves. We complicate life with our contradictions and inconsistencies with truth. We give up freedom when we live against the truth of who we are. To resonate as truth is to live free.

In truth, we are free of the divisive thoughts that keep us stuck in conflict. We clearly see true from false. We see the false in greed and competition and end our fight against others. In our duality mindset, we live in conflict. Where there is conflict, there is suffering. In our resonance with truth, we live in cooperation with others. We live in peace and unity.

In our fragmented lives, we mistake truth for strong attractions. We resonate with those who have similar fragmented parts of their lives and see fragmentation as truth. We accept conflict for its place as safety and lose sight of truth. In truth, we see beyond an attraction for its fragmented resonant frequency. We see the false in our feelings of familiarity.

In our resonance with truth, we see balance in all areas of our lives. We are healthy in mind, body, and spirit. Our relationships flow. We live joyfully on purpose and share our truth with the collective. In our truth, we feel a deep inner knowing that guides us on a path of integrity. We live in resonance with truth.

In our resonance with truth, we feel a deep sense of safety and belonging. We are aligned with universal order and feel one with all. We feel a symbiotic relationship as being mutually beneficial for transmitting and receiving information. We feel safe in our connection. We feel supported and that we belong as we resonate with unity.

To resonate with truth is to feel a depth of gratitude. It is a feeling that does not build on previous knowledge or experience. It is a deep inner feeling that is felt with our entire being. We feel our connection with the entire universe as a deep sense of freedom. We feel appreciation for our connection and are grateful to be alive.

In our alignment with truth, we are in resonance with our true nature. There is freedom from the restrictions of emotional pain and struggle. We feel completely safe, supported, and loved in life. We are true to ourselves and feel truth as a deep sense of freedom. In our truth, we are in alignment with the light that we are. We resonate as truth and live truth.

Transformed Resonance

Is the transformation of our resonance the end of our healing? We see and feel balance in all areas of our lives. We feel peace and know that our emotional attachments have ended. Divisive thoughts turn to peace. It is in the dissolving of our ego-structures that our balanced expressions show resonance transformation. We *feel* transformed.

To transform our resonance is to bring balance to fragmentation. It is in the fragmented areas of our lives that we see disorder. In our balanced resonance, we see and feel balance. We live in truth and life flows. We resonate as peace and therefore resonate with others in peace. Our resonant frequency aligns with order. To be transformed is to feel whole.

Feeling transformed and in balance involves continued healing. Our emotional transformation is an exploration to transform our pain. There are no peaks of enlightenment to a point where we are finished with our healing work. As long as we are human, we will experience emotional challenges. In our awareness, we stay on our healing path.

To live transformed is to continue to dissolve conditioned structures. A transformed being expresses truth as truth and sees arrogance as a conflict with truth. We see our ego as a tool to navigate through life while we treat others and ourselves with kindness. All divisiveness is known to be a hindrance to our freedom. We express our resonance transformation as truth.

We transform our resonance to end our pain and suffering. To live transformed is to know that our emotional attachments have ended because emotional struggle has ended. We align with the frequencies of balanced memories as our being is in resonance with balance. Our balanced frequency is reflected in our emotions, health, and relationships. We live in peace.

Living transformed is living truth. It is living in alignment with the true nature of our being. We align with truth and let it guide us through life. We know we are always on the right path because we are in alignment with truth. It is in truth that we stay true to ourselves.

To live transformed holds a profound responsibility. It is to live in the truth of our transformation with the knowing of our one shared awareness. Our thoughts and actions matter as they reverberate into the collective memory. To live transformed is to know in depth that our emotional transformation is shared with all.

In our awareness we live transformed. To live transformed is to see our conditioned perception fall away as we see through the lens of truth. We are aware of fragmentation in disguise and we stay with truth. We live in the light of our truth and resonate with truth. We feel the freedom of our transformation.

Transforming our resonance is the beginning of true healing. The peace and freedom we feel in our lives opens us up to continuing our healing work. We stand in the resonance of truth and live truth. We express ourselves as balanced beings as we live aware of the true nature of our being. We live transformed.

CHAPTER 20

Freedom in Depth

TRUE FREEDOM IS NOT bound by limitations. To feel freedom in depth is to see beyond all definitions and practices. It is to stand sovereign in a world of control and organized groups. In freedom, we live in peace and in the flow of life. We feel our universal connection as our entire being feels freedom as gratitude, forgiveness, knowing, and love. It is *true* freedom in depth.

Freedom in depth is a deep knowing that is felt with our entire being. We feel forgiveness without expectations and gratitude for all of life. The light that we are radiates as we feel a depth of love that cannot be challenged. It is in our awareness that we know freedom and feel it as truth. True freedom has no limiting factors.

We feel the depth of freedom within. There are no limitations to restrict freedom in depth. There are no walls to hold us back from feeling free. We see beyond the opposite of confinement as being the definition of freedom. It is in the depth of our being that we feel an opening that connects us with all life. It is where we feel free to feel freedom.

To feel depth of freedom is to live in the flow of life. We live free of control and the limits of organized groups. We follow nothing but our inner knowing. We know freedom with our entire being. We stand in our truth and power and live free. In our freedom, we live without fear of uncertainty and we are open to change.

In the depth of freedom, we feel a deep sense of security. We feel held and supported by the universe and live with a depth of gratitude. The depth of freedom as gratitude comes without practice. We feel gratitude as an extension of our universal connection. It is purely genuine. We feel grateful to be alive and in our connection. In the depth of freedom, we feel safe and in peace.

In our freedom, we are not restricted by emotional attachments. We stand outside of our relationships, beliefs, material possessions, group affiliations, and social statuses and we feel filled with peace and security. We see emotional attachments as a false sense of security and we know that we have refuge in our truth. We live in the flow of life and feel free.

In the depth of freedom we are free from harbored guilt and resentments. We feel forgiveness for those whom we felt had caused us pain. We forgive without an attachment to an outcome or hope for a specific feeling. Depth of forgiveness happens when we open our hearts and feel our connection with the entire universal collective. Forgiveness for one is forgiveness for all.

We feel freedom in depth as a depth of knowing. It is a knowing that goes beyond intuition or wisdom. In our awareness, we have access to a language that is innate to all.

We take information in as feelings and images and we are aware of the meanings instantaneously. All our senses are awakened to help guide us on our free path of truth.

True freedom is living without limitations. We stand free in our truth and power and live in the flow of life. In the depth of freedom, we feel and know freedom with our entire being. We live in peace and feel freedom as gratitude, forgiveness, knowing, and love. It is in the depth of our being that we feel a connection with all of life. It is a depth of knowing that we are free.

Depth of Knowing

To know is limited to learned information. We know only what we have learned through others and our experiences. To know in depth goes beyond knowledge passed on from others or from acquired understanding. Depth of knowing is an innate intelligence that opens in our awareness. We are free to know in depth.

Depth of knowing comes through pure awareness. It is a knowing beyond intuition, which is often muddied by previous thoughts. We feel a deep knowing that cannot be denied as it is awakened through all our senses. In the depth of knowing we are aware of the information that we align with. We are open and receptive to knowing.

In the depth of knowing, we are free to know truth. Our knowing guides us even when there are physical limitations to our senses. There is a deep knowing that is known within that is free of all limitations. To know in depth is to live in our truth and be the knowing that we know in depth. It is to live in the freedom of truth.

Knowing in depth is to live aware. Our awareness is

hindered by poor diet, poor habits, constant work, and increasing emotional troubles. To live with depth of knowing is to have clarity of being and to live through that clarity. In our awareness, we bring balance to imbalances in our lives. We feel into our being and know in depth what needs to be done.

Knowing in depth opens to order. We see needed order in areas of our lives where we listen to our truth and we act without resistance. In depth of knowing, when we see disorder, we simply make the needed changes without hesitation. To know in depth is to live in alignment with order.

In the depth of knowing, we express ourselves through our heart. We feel our universal connection and extend kindness to all. Division turns into unification as we replace competition with cooperation. We know in depth that we are all one and see the futility in fighting others as going against ourselves. In depth of knowing, we feel a deep love for the entire collective.

To know in depth is a profound feeling of freedom. We see and feel freedom in areas of our lives where there used to be emotional blocks. We live through freedom, as life flows. In depth of knowing, we see resistance and we live without denial or with any attempt to control outcomes. We live in the flow of life, free and in peace.

Knowing in depth comes through our shared awareness. We align with all memory, as we align with the frequency that we are. Every word spoken and action through time is available to us. To know in depth is to be respectful for what we transmit while being grateful for what we receive. It is to truly know the true nature of our being.

The only limitation to knowing in depth is our own restraint. We have access to all universal memory. We know with our entire being what is true in depth. It is in the depth of knowing that we live as the awareness that we are. In our depth of knowing, we feel freedom through our shared connection. To know in depth is to be aligned with the light that we are.

Depth of Forgiveness

To feel depth of forgiveness is to feel freedom. We are free of emotional attachments with open hearts. Love is extended to the entire collective, as we feel connected to all. To forgive in depth is to be free of holding expectations or controlling outcomes. We are free of judgments, guilt, and resentments. We are in peace. Depth of forgiveness is to feel freedom as love.

Depth of forgiveness is an extension of our open hearts. In true love, we are free of restriction to hold back on forgiving. It is natural to forgive because we *are* love. We feel a profound sense of freedom to forgive and we do it without effort. It is in our shared awareness that we feel the truest form of forgiveness as love.

To feel forgiveness in depth is to refrain from expectations. Depth of forgiveness is unconditional. We are free of expecting a resulting feeling from forgiving. The outcome is left to the flow of life. To insert desires and probabilities limits our freedom. In truth, we feel a free and open feeling for all of life. We are free of attachments and expectations with our hearts open.

In the depth of forgiveness, we feel peace. We are free of resentment because we know in depth that it restricts our freedom. It is through the healing of our emotions that we feel forgiveness, regardless of poor behavior of others or ourselves. Hate, anger, shame, or blame cannot live in the light of our truth. In the depth of forgiveness, we live in peace.

Living through our truth as depth of forgiveness, we are free of judgment. To judge is to live through a divisive perception and see others as separate while being fast to find fault. In the freedom of forgiveness, we are free of seeing right or wrong. We see everyone and thing as part of divine creation. In the depth of forgiveness, we feel united as one.

Feeling forgiveness in depth is to be emotionally balanced. We are free of emotional pain and attachments and our peace within is extended out to all. We are free of manipulating factors to feel peace. We feel peace first and then we feel forgiveness. To be in depth of forgiveness is to be free of emotional restrictions. We live free.

In depth of forgiveness, we know in depth that forgiveness for one is forgiveness for all. We know that holding back forgiveness hinders the evolution of the entire collective. In depth of forgiveness, we see clearly that we are all seeing through our emotions. In our awareness, we see that forgiveness is not limited to one individual. We are contributing to our one conscious mind.

To feel depth of forgiveness is to feel compassion for others. We feel compassion as love for ourselves extended out. It is to know in depth that we are all connected and it is futile to be against others only to be against ourselves. We feel love in our hearts, as forgiveness is conveyed to the entire collective, as true love.

In the freedom of forgiveness, we are in peace. We are clear of all emotional restrictions and feel love for all life. We are in peace regardless of past experiences. We live in the flow of life and we are free of judgments, guilt, and resentments.

Forgiveness in depth is peace unfolded into love for all. We feel forgiveness for others as we feel forgiven.

Depth of Gratitude

Depth of gratitude is freedom in depth. We are in alignment with the universe and feel its perfection. We feel safe and protected with a deep sense of belonging. We feel one with the whole and that life is always working for our benefit. Synchronicities are common and we know the meanings in depth. In the depth of gratitude, we are deeply grateful with our hearts open.

Depth of gratitude is an alignment of unification with universal order. Feeling gratitude in depth happens without a disciplined practice. We feel gratitude without expectations for a happier emotional being or to receive anything in return. Depth of gratitude is being aligned with the truth of all life. It is felt in the awareness of our shared awareness.

In depth of gratitude, our awareness is sharp. We are aware of all the significant synchronicities that show us life is working in our favor. We feel deeply grateful for the smallest of signs as we flow with all incoming information. We see resistance as going against ourselves and we stay true to the flow. Depth of gratitude is being open to truth.

To feel depth of gratitude is to feel a deep sense of safety and belonging. We feel protected and move through life without fear or hesitation. We feel held by the universe and that we belong everywhere. It is in this truth that we know in depth that we are a part of a unified field of awareness. We know we are safe in the light of truth.

In depth of gratitude, we feel freedom. We are free of emotional attachments and see our life unfold with indescribable peace. We are free of suffering from past traumatic experiences and are deeply grateful for the freedom that we feel. We are no longer stuck and feel gratitude in depth. We are free to feel grateful.

In the freedom of depth of gratitude, we live without division, competition, and greed. We feel our connection as one and are grateful for one and all. We see the pettiness in opposing others, fighting for who is better, and the constant hunger for more. In the depth of gratitude, we feel grateful for the little things in life as well as the big. We are grateful for everything.

In the depth of gratitude, we are deeply grateful with a depth of love. It is in the depth of freedom that love is extended out as gratitude. We feel grateful for everyone, as we know that we are all connected. We feel the love of our shared awareness and we feel grateful to be alive. Depth of gratitude is felt as an abundance of love that can bring us to tears. It is truth as love.

The feeling of gratitude in depth is without expectations to feel peace. We *are* peace. Gratitude lives though us and it shows as life reflects the frequency that we are. We see open doors where there were blocks. We feel peace where there was pain. In the depth of gratitude, we flow with life. We live free and are deeply grateful.

To live through depth of gratitude is living without effort to be grateful. We feel naturally grateful in the unity of our shared awareness. We feel protected as one with the whole. We feel that we belong. We see fragmented areas of our lives come together in perfect order and are grateful in depth. It is in the depth of gratitude that we feel life as an abundance of love.

Depth of Love

Depth of love is to live without conditions and emotional restrictions. In the awareness of our shared awareness, we see *everyone* as love. We feel protected and that we belong everywhere. We are free of all limitations to our freedom. We know in depth that desires, fears, jealousy, and control are devoid of love. To feel depth of love is to *be* love and radiate love to all.

The depth of love is an expansion of the heart. We live through the light that we are as love. To be the love that we are is to see love everywhere. Depth of love is seen and felt without exclusions. Everyone is included in the love that we are. In love, we live without hate or divisiveness. Division cannot live in the depth of love.

To live in the depth of love is to love others in depth. Depth of love is a deep feeling of compassion for another being. We see others as one with the whole and feel love for others as part of ourselves. We filter poor behavior through our heart and feel depth of forgiveness as we know we are all seeing through our emotions. It is to feel true love.

To feel the truth of depth of love is to be aware of blocks to love. We know in depth that hate cannot live up to love in depth. We see any opposition to being in the love that we are as living against the flow of life. We see expectations of love as a hindrance to the truth of love. To live with depth of love is to radiate the love that we are.

Depth of love is free of suffering. We hold no attachments or expectations. We live through the truth of love and see our emotions in balance. Love in depth is always balancing and in the truth of love we see order. We feel peace as the love that we are. In depth of love, we are in alignment with all life as love. Suffering dissolves in the light of our love.

To live as the light of our love is to be in the awareness of our shared awareness. We feel supported, safe, and loved. We feel connected as one awareness, one love. To feel depth of love is to feel a deep sense of belonging. We feel an abundance of energy as love and feel one with everyone and thing. We feel freedom in depth as love.

In the depth of love, we share peace in our relationships. There is an energy exchange that is free of barter or the need to balance out the deeds of another. We live through the truth of love that we are. Our relationships flow without fear, jealousy, desires, or control. We live free of painful restrictions. We live through the depth of love, whether alone or in relation with another.

Living in the freedom of depth as love is to feel love as freedom. We feel open and love every living being as love. We feel love for the birds and bees. We feel connected to the sky above and the mycelium below, and everything in between. There are no limiting factors in the depth of love. We love as a feeling of being united with all.

In the depth of love, we unite together with all as one love. We see everyone as love. We feel free, open, and connected. We feel safe and supported. It is in the awareness of our universal connection that our entire being feels freedom as gratitude, forgiveness, knowing, and love. We live as love and feel true freedom in depth.

CHAPTER 21

In Our Light

IN THE TIMELESSNESS OF light, we know in depth what is true. Our minds have been purified and we are living free of darkness. We feel the power of the light beings that we are. We live in the light of our truth and constantly integrate truth into our awareness. In our light, we are free of ego-structures that separate us. We live united in light as the light beings that we are.

In our light, we are free of space and time. Light travels in a flash and is not bound by dimensions. To resonate with the power of light is to be in resonance with all life. We are separated only by our minds. To live as the light beings that we are is to maintain our resonance with light. It is to shine our light through whatever our form.

To live as the light that we are is to know in depth that we are united as one. We live as our light and not as the ego-structures that separate us. In our light, we engage in relationships without division and activism, without resistance. We live together and are united in freedom. We feel our connection with everyone as one with the whole. We live as our light.

To live in our light is to live free of darkness. It is to live with purity of thought and to constantly integrate truth into our emotional healing. We live in awareness and own, feel, name, express, and face our pain. In our light, we live free of emotional attachments and patterns that pull us into the dark. We live free as light.

In the freedom of our light, we stand in our truth and power. We stand in our power and are guided by truth. We feel truth and power as freedom and live free of restrictions. To live in the freedom of our light is to radiate truth and power as our light. We live without searching for freedom because in our light, we are free.

In the intelligence of our light, we live as free as light. We live as light without bounds. We are free of emotional attachments to people, places, and material possessions. In our light, we are free of life being limited to space and time. We live in peace and in the flow of life. We live as the infinite light beings that we are. We live as our truth.

Living as the truth of our light is to live true to our being. In our light, we know in depth what is true and we stay true to that knowing. We remain open to our light without being caught in the divisive chaos of society. In the light of our truth, we live free of division. Truth dissolves all fallacies and we live free as light and united as one. We live in the power of our truth.

In our light, we go beyond the limitations of the ego. We transcend our ego-structures, while being grounded in the present. We unite with the universe as one and radiate divine light. Our hearts are open and we feel connected with all of life. In our light, we are in peace and feel supported by the universe. We live aware of the light beings that we are.

To live in the truth of our light is to live in freedom. We are in peace while being fully awake. We live in the light of our truth and stand grounded in our power. We live free of darkness as division and emotional restriction. In our light, we feel our universal connection and we live united in light as the light beings that we are.

We Are Light

Is it a coincidence that we feel uplifted in light? We are beings of nature and light is manifested in all of nature. In the intelligence of light, we see our dreams and visions illuminated. We see that our inner light is one with divine light. As light, we resonate with the energetic vibrations of another. We are drawn to light and feel restored from light. We *are* light.

As the light beings that we are, we feel connected to light. We feel motivated to go outside on sunny days and healthier after a day outside in the sun. We see light as superior to darkness as we speak in metaphors to go toward the light and to shine our inner light. It is light that uplifts our spirits in moments of despair. Light is divine in its true nature.

Light is timeless. In light, there is only the present. It is in our light that we see truth in a flash and our problems are dissolved in the speed of light. We live free of the restrictions of time and we flow with life. It is in our awareness that we see ourselves as one ever-present light. We know in depth that we are light.

In the awareness of our light, we are not bound to dimensions. We feel free and open for life to unfold with its boundless potential. We do not get stuck in problems or confused about our next direction. We remember the light that we are and we live through our light. We feel freedom deeply because light is equal to freedom.

Light is intelligent in its infinite connection with all nature. We absorb the light from the sun and receive physiological benefits. We take in energy from plants that are dependent on sunlight for growth. Our bodies synchronize with the light of our planet for balanced health. As light beings, we are in connection with all nature. We are one light.

In our light, we see truth. We see our inner light illuminated as dreams and visions. We falsely separate our inner light from divine light, but they are united together as one. We know that there are deeper meanings to the light that we see illuminated as visual images in our minds. It is in our truth that we know in depth that we are light.

Light is love in its infinite nature. We feel drawn to light because we feel its presence. We are attracted to beauty as love when we resonate with its frequency. In our light, we feel a deep connection with all of life, as love. We radiate light as love and compassion for all. As the light that we are, we *are* love.

To be in our light is to be in unity with all light. We feel one with the sun, stars, and rainbows. We bathe in the light of the sun, gaze at the stars shining in the night, and stand in awe at the colors arched in the sky refracted from raindrops. We view light as a wonder. We feel drawn to light because we are light beings.

As the true light beings that we are, we are timeless. We live free of the emotional boundaries of life as we see truth through the truth of our light. We live free of the restrictions of time and see our infinite potential. In the awareness of our light, we resonate with divine light. We feel the love that we are and our connection to all. We live as the light that we are.

Living in Darkness

In the darkness of our minds, we hold our ego-structures in fear of light. Our emotional attachments burn with intensity as we stay stuck in our pain. Time slows as our problems become magnified and we become imprisoned in time. In the dark, we get caught in the false light of the ego and avoid the freedom of light. We live in the dark.

Living in darkness is not the opposite of living in light. We need the dark to open to light and we need light to intercept darkness. We need the cycles of day and night to live in balance. It is our trapped dark emotional pain that keeps us stuck in a state of suffering. In our suffering, we live in darkness. We avoid the light.

Living in fear of light is avoiding the true freedom of light. In our darkness, we stay within the borders of our false securities. We avoid venturing into the light because it would take away our associated ego identity. We hold on to the known while unaware of the loss of our freedom. It is in our truth that we see light. In our fear of light, we remain in the dark.

In our darkness, we see through the false light of the ego. The ego shines brightly with grandiosity as our hidden emotional pain burns strong. Our ego shines brighter as our ego-structures turn away from true light. In the darkness of our pain, we hold our ego-structures in place because we cannot handle the intensity of true light.

In darkness, light seems far away. We are bound to time with all its complexities. We hold emotional attachments and expectations that restrict our freedom. Life becomes increasingly difficult in the dark. We let societal structures drag us down and we stay stuck in patterns that pull us further into the dark. We think that light is out of reach, but we *are* light.

Living in darkness is living against light as our truth. We live in defiance of our true nature and values. We blame others for our challenges and feel victim to our circumstances. We wait for the government or a higher power to take our struggles away. It is in the dark that we live powerless. We go against the true nature of our being. We go against our light.

In the darkness of our minds, we see division instead of unity. We live in conflict with others and ourselves. Our thoughts get twisted into believing that we are separate, so we compete and fight for who is better. We judge and use words to inflict pain while unaware that we are all connected. We live divided in our darkness. In the truth of our light, we are all one.

To live in darkness is to give up the true freedom of light. In our suffering we feel stuck in time with our problems magnified. We become absorbed by darkness instead of engaging in the freedom of light. We miss out on living free and feel trapped in life. In our darkness, we exchange freedom for suffering. In our light, we live free, as light shining.

Darkness wanes in the face of light. Living free of darkness is to transcend our fears through truth and dissolve our ego-structures. It is to recognize darkness as a hindrance to our freedom. In our light, we flow with time and live without emotional restrictions. In our freedom, we shine the true light of our being. We live in the light of our truth.

Living in Our Light

To live in our light is to live in truth. It is to always be aware of our light and integrate truth into our awareness. In our light, we live in space and time as our light. We live free of emotional attachments, fears, and expectations that restrict our freedom. We feel universal unity and extend light as love to all. Living in our light is to be the light that we are.

Living in the light of our truth is to live truth. In our light, we live in peace because we are aware of resistance being in contradiction to our truth. Living as our light is to continue our emotional healing work and to be open to changing our beliefs. We are guided by truth and stand in the power of our truth. To live in our light is to stand true to ourselves.

To live in light is to feel true freedom. We are free of emotional restrictions and live in the flow of life. We do not try to control outcomes because we are free of fears and expectations. In the freedom of light, we are not bound by limitations. We are open to change. Freedom as light is felt with our entire being. It is in our light that we live free as light.

In our light, we live in the present. We are focused and grounded, as we know the past and future as the present. We are not stuck in the pain of the past or searching for an answer from the future. All we need is known within the light of our being. We know in depth that our truth is light, so we live as the light that we are.

In our light, we are in alignment with our innate power. We stand in the power of our light and hold no other power above ours. In the connection of our light, we connect with all that we need to know. We are guided by truth as power and live in the light of our power. In the power of our light, we resonate with our light and stand true to the power of light that we are.

In our light, we know in depth that light is not equal to increased ego identity. It is in our light that we feel true power as light. Our ego-structures as we know them dissolve and we live free. We feel the freedom of light and radiate true light from our being. In our light, we are free of the walls of conditioning that separate us. We live in our light and are free of limitations.

Living in our light is to live open to our light. We feel a deep sense of safety and belonging, so we feel free and open. In our light, we live in the freedom of our universal connection. We live free of emotional restrictions that close us down. It is in our light that we live free of the uncertainties of life. We are open to the unfolding of life and live as light beings.

To live as our light is to be love. We radiate compassion in the light of love for all. We inspire others to open to light as we all share one universal light. In our light as love, we see unity, instead of separation. We are in alignment with all life. We are one light and we shine brighter together when we stand true to the light that we are.

Living in our light is truth radiated. We are aware and live true to the light beings that we are. We are not held down in the darkness with emotional restrictions of the past and future. We live free in the present as light. We feel our light as love and extend it to the entire collective. We live in our light, unified with all as one light.

United in Light

We have journeyed through our emotional pain and opened to our light. Our endings became our freedom. Our pain has turned to love. It is in the awareness of our light that we feel safe and open. We see others and ourselves as divine light and know in depth that we are one light. We live as interconnected light beings. We live united in light.

In our light, we live as one light. We are aware of our individuality, while knowing we are all connected. We see the divine light in all and live free of division. We see others and ourselves without a preconceived perception. We live together in light without judgment and conflict. We live united as the light that we are.

To live united in light is to live truth. We have opened to our light through our suffering and live as the true light that we are. We see others as the same light but going through his or her individual journey to open to our one light. It is in our light that we stand true to ourselves and see truth in others. In the light of our truth, we stand united in light.

In our light, we feel safe and open. We feel our connection with the entire universal collective and feel safe, supported, and loved. Fears transcend through truth and dissolve in the speed of light. We live in our awareness as being unified with all. We see the light of others and live in the openness of our unified light.

In the openness of our light, we feel free. We have ended our emotional attachments and feel a true sense of freedom. The freedom from our restrictions has opened us to feeling connected to all life. We feel freedom at the depth of our being and grateful for life. We feel in resonance with light. It is in our light that we feel freedom as light.

In our light, we live in peace. We feel one with all and completely unified as peace. We feel peace without effort and connected without conflict. We live as a fearless light being in peace and our peace is extended to others. In our light, we feel united with all as the peace that we are. We see others and ourselves as one light.

In our light, we live as interconnected light beings. We feel a love in depth for all. We feel the truth of love. In the light of our love, we know in depth that we are one light as one love. We see others as love and feel love for others as part of ourselves. In our light, we live through the truth of who we are. We live united as love and light.

We live united in light and see others as the same light. We live in alignment with all life as light. We shine the light that we are but know in depth that we shine brighter together. In our light, we feel our infinite connection, as a universal family united in light. It is in our light that we live in the freedom of our light united as one.

We have transformed our awareness and opened to our light. We are free of painful restrictions and feel our light as a depth of love for all. We see others and ourselves as divine light. In our light, we live united in our universal connection. We live in our light as the light beings that we are. It is as our light that we have come home as one light.

EPILOGUE

To Remember

IN OUR SEARCH FOR freedom from suffering, we get caught trying. Emotional memory repeats in its attempt to balance. It is in the recognition of our true nature that we live in the balance of our peace. It is that which is known in us and is unshakable in the midst of chaos. Our known suffering lives in our minds, which forget truth. To know freedom is to remember.

Our lives are built on conditioning. We have learned how to forget the truth of who we are to become a person of acquired knowledge. We do not have to find or become the awareness that we are, because it is our true nature. There is a very fine veil between the ignorance of our truth and pure awareness. Our conditioning falls away in our remembrance.

To remember our true nature is only the beginning of living our truth. We will continue to shed our ways of being that we built our lives around. We notice emotional behaviors and diffuse them as fast as they come. The recognition of our true nature has us living with good morals and no fears or temptations. We stand in truth and live truth.

In the remembrance of our being, our emotional attachments fall away. We no longer hold hollow desires that are clearly only placeholders to fill a feeling of lack. We feel so filled with love that our lives reflect the love that we are. We see truth come through every area of our lives. We live free of the suffering that is a result of emotional attachments.

In our freedom, emotional memory balances. In our remembrance, we still see our memories as a part of our story, but we are not shaken emotionally. We are free of the repetition of our memory working toward balance. Memory remains in balance without emotional attachments. We live in peace.

To live without suffering is to be in peace with all experiences. Life will always bring challenges that are out of our control, but it is how we react to life that keeps us in balance. We can always go back to the deep knowing of our true nature and know in depth that we are not our experiences. We are pure, conscious, ever-present awareness that witnesses them.

We live as the light of our being connected to all as one light. We do not live as our body or a mind of thoughts that are associated with separation. We live a life that is in the goodness of all. We live as individual beings of memory that are part of a vast field of memory. We may have differences of mind and thought, but in remembering, we never see through a lens of division.

Living a life of truth is living a selfless life. We feel love in our hearts and extend love through our being. We share our life as a benefit to the collective, whatever our service. We are aware that our thoughts, emotions, and actions are part of one greater mind and memory. It is in our depth of knowing that we are contributing to something limitless.

In the recognition of the true nature of our being, we suffer no more. Emotional memory heals and we live in freedom as the peace of our being. Our minds are pure and our beings are in balance. We see that we are one light and we live in the light of that truth. We live in the depth of knowing that we are ever-present awareness illuminated. To remember is to never forget.

ACKNOWLEDGMENTS

T O ALL THOSE WHO triggered emotional pain in me, thank you. If it were not for the pain and suffering, I would not have learned what I needed for growth. I am now more resilient because of it all.

Eric, thank you for everything. There are no additional words that can describe my gratitude.

Thank you, Donna, Elisabeth, Kelly and Erin. I appreciate you all.

Thank you to all the readers who step into this work and are willing to make the changes in their personal lives and in this world.

ENDNOTES

Introduction

1. Vedanta Society of New York. "39. Katha Upanishad | Mantra 2.3.1 | Swami Sarvapriyananda," January 27, 2023. https://www.youtube.com/watch?v=-nVuiTjIzqs.

PART I
Chapter 1

1. National Institute of Mental Health (NIMH). "Major Depression," n.d. https://www.nimh.nih.gov/health/statistics/major-depression.
2. "Cancer Data and Statistics | CDC," n.d. https://www.cdc.gov/cancer/dcpc/data/.
3. Centers for Disease Control and Prevention. "Obesity Is a Common, Serious, and Costly Disease," July 20, 2022. https://www.cdc.gov/obesity/data/adult.html.
4. Wang, Fushun, Jiongjiong Yang, Fang Pan, Roger C.M. Ho, and Jason H. Huang. "Editorial: Neurotransmitters and Emotions." *Frontiers in Psychology* 11 (January 29, 2020). https://doi.org/10.3389/fpsyg.2020.00021.

5. Sheldrake, Rupert. "Extended Mind, Power, & Prayer." *Psychological Perspectives*, March 1, 1988. https://doi.org/10.1080/00332928808408771.

6. Rupert Sheldrake. "Morphic Resonance and Morphic Fields: An Introduction," n.d. https://www.sheldrake.org/research/morphic-resonance/introduction.

Chapter 2

1. Felitti, Vincent J., Robert F. Anda, Dale Nordenberg, David P. Williamson, Alison M. Spitz, Valerie J. Edwards, Mary P. Koss, and James G. Marks. "Relationship of Childhood Abuse and Household Dysfunction to Many of the Leading Causes of Death in Adults." *American Journal of Preventive Medicine* 14, no. 4 (May 1, 1998): 245–58. https://doi.org/10.1016/s0749-3797(98)00017-8.

2. Song, Huan, Fang Fang, Gunnar Tomasson, Filip K. Arnberg, David Mataix-Cols, Lorena Fernández De La Cruz, Catarina Almqvist, Katja Fall, and Unnur Valdimarsdóttir. "Association of Stress-Related Disorders with Subsequent Autoimmune Disease." JAMA 319, no. 23 (June 19, 2018): 2388. https://doi.org/10.1001/jama.2018.7028.

Chapter 3

1. Mu-ming Poo, Michele Pignatelli, Tomás J. Ryan, Susumu Tonegawa, Tobias Bonhoeffer, Kelsey C. Martin, Andrii Rudenko, et al., "What Is Memory? The Present State of the Engram." *BMC Biology* 14, no. 1 (May 19, 2016). https://doi.org/10.1186/s12915-016-0261-6.

2. Svoboda, Elizabeth, "Light-Triggered Genes Reveal Hidden Workings of Memory." *Quanta Magazine* (May 18, 2020). https://www.quantamagazine.org/light-triggered-genes-reveal-the-hidden-workings-of-memory-20171214/.

3. Svoboda, "Light-Triggered Genes."

4. Saplakoglu, Yasemin, "Mitochondria Double as Tiny Lenses in the Eye." *Quanta Magazine* (April 06, 2022). https://www.quantamagazine.org/mitochondria-double-as-tiny-lenses-in-the-eye-20220405/.

5. Saplakoglu, "Mitochondria Double as Tiny Lenses in the Eye."

6. Korotkov. "Prof. Fritz-Albert Popp." IUMAB, April 24, 2019. https://www.iumab.org/prof-fritz-albert-popp/.

7. International Institute of Biophysics. Health Angel Foundation. "Dr. Fritz-Albert Popp. About the Coherence of Biophotons." April 22, 2023. https://www.meridianenergies.net/wp-content/uploads/2012/04/CoherenceOfBiophotons.pdf

8. Biontology Arizona. "Dr. Popp Biophoton Theory | Fritz-Albert Popp | GermanPhysicist Popp | BiontologyArizona," June 5, 2018. https://biontologyarizona.com/dr-fritz-albert-popp/.

Chapter 4

1. David A. Sbarra and Paul J. Nietert. "Divorce and Death: Forty Years of the Charleston Heart Study." *Psychological Science* 20, no. 1 (2009): 107–13. https://doi.org/10.1111/j.1467-9280.2008.02252.x.

2. National Institute on Drug Abuse. "Treatment and Recovery | National Institute on Drug Abuse," March 9, 2023. https://nida.nih.gov/publications/drugs-brains-behavior-science-addiction/treatment-recovery.

Chapter 5

1. "Stress in America," n.d. https://www.apa.org/news/press/releases/stress/2022/march-2022-survival-mode.

2. "Stress in America."

3.   Charles J. Holahan, Rudolf H. Moos, Carole K. Holahan, Penny L. Brennan, and Kathleen K. Schutte. "Stress Generation, Avoidance Coping, and Depressive Symptoms: A 10-Year Model." *Journal of Consulting and Clinical Psychology* 73, no. 4 (January 1, 2005): 658–66. https://doi.org/10.1037/0022-006x.73.4.658.

Chapter 6

1.   "Depressive Disorder (Depression)." World Health Organization. Accessed April 23, 2023. https://www.who.int/news-room/fact-sheets/detail/depression/.
2.   "Covid-19 Pandemic Triggers 25% Increase in Prevalence of Anxiety and Depression Worldwide." World Health Organization. https://www.who.int/news/item/02-03-2022-covid-19-pandemic-triggers-25-increase-in-prevalence-of-anxiety-and-depression-worldwide.
3.   Korotkov. "Prof. Fritz-Albert Popp."

PART II
Chapter 7

1.   Bioregulatory Medicine | BRMI Bioregulatory Medicine Institute. "BRMI | History—Pierre Jacques Antoine Béchamp," n.d. https://www.biologicalmedicineinstitute.com/antoine-bechamp.
2.   Schwartz, Lisa, and Steven Woloshin. "Medical Marketing in the United States, 1997–2016." *JAMA* 321, no. 1 (January 1, 2019): 80. https://doi.org/10.1001/jama.2018.19320.
3.   Shmerling, Robert H., MD. "Harvard Health Ad Watch: How Direct-to-Consumer Ads Hook Us." *Harvard Health*, March 3, 2022. https://www.health.harvard.edu/blog/harvard-health-ad-watch-what-you-should-know-about-direct-to-consumer-ads-2019092017848.
4.   "Industrial Sugar Market Size, Share & Growth | Forecast

[2029]," n.d. https://www.fortunebusinessinsights.com/industrial-sugar-market-102462.

5. Centers for Disease Control and Prevention. "Obesity Is a Common, Serious, and Costly Disease."

6. "National Diabetes Statistics Report | Diabetes | CDC," n.d. https://www.cdc.gov/diabetes/data/statistics-report/index.html.

Chapter 8

1. "Stress in America 2020: A National Mental Health Crisis," n.d. https://www.apa.org/news/press/releases/stress/2020/report-october.

2. CCHR International. "Number of People Taking Psychiatric Drugs in the United States | The Mental Health Industry Watchdog," May 13, 2023. https://www.cchrint.org/psychiatric-drugs/people-taking-psychiatric-drugs/.

3. Puderbaugh, Matt, and Prabhu D. Emmady. "Neuroplasticity." StatPearls Publishing, 2015.

4. Singer, Emily. "The Maestro of Memory Manipulation." *Quanta Magazine*. February 1, 2019. https://www.quantamagazine.org/the-maestro-of-memory-manipulation-20160623/.

5. Puderbaugh and Emmady, "Neuroplasticity."

6. Harvard Medical School. "Depression and Alzheimer's," August 9, 2019. https://hms.harvard.edu/news/depression-alzheimers.

7. The HighWire. "Aluminum Expert Unearths Likely Cause of Alzheimer's." July 21, 2023. https://thehighwire.com/ark-videos/aluminum-expert-unearths-likely-cause-of-alzheimers/.

Chapter 9

1. Masaru Emoto. *The Healing Power of Water*. Hay House, 2008.
2. Kramer, Achim, Tanja Lange, Claudia Spies, Anna-Marie Finger, Daniela Berg, and Henrik Oster. "Foundations of Circadian Medicine." *PLOS Biology* 20, no. 3 (March 24, 2022): e3001567. https://doi.org/10.1371/journal.pbio.3001567.
3. Kramer, Lange, Spies, Finger, Berg, and Oster. "Foundations of Circadian Medicine."
4. Schernhammer, Eva S., Francine Laden, Frank E. Speizer, Walter C. Willett, David J. Hunter, Ichiro Kawachi, Charles S. Fuchs, and Graham A. Colditz. "Night-Shift Work and Risk of Colorectal Cancer in the Nurses' Health Study." *Journal of the National Cancer Institute* 95, no. 11 (June 4, 2003): 825–28. https://doi.org/10.1093/jnci/95.11.825.
5. Kramer, Lange, Spies, Finger, Berg, and Oster. "Foundations of Circadian Medicine."

Chapter 10

1. Geoengineering Watch. "Geoengineering Affects You, Your Environment, and Your Loved Ones," June 14, 2023. https://www.geoengineeringwatch.org/.
2. Mapes, Lynda V. "Drugs Found in Puget Sound Salmon from Tainted Wastewater." *The Seattle Times*, February 25, 2016. https://www.seattletimes.com/seattle-news/environment/drugs-flooding-into-puget-sound-and-its-salmon/; Mapes, Lynda V. "Puget Sound Salmon Do Drugs, Which May Hurt Their Survival." *The Seattle Times*, April 9, 2018. https://www.seattletimes.com/seattle-news/environment/puget-sound-salmon-do-drugs-which-may-hurt-their-survival/; Romo, Vanessa. "Traces of Opioids Found in Seattle-Area Mussels." *NPR*,

May 26, 2018. https://www.npr.org/sections/thet-wo-way/2018/05/25/614593382/traces-of-opioids-found-in-seattle-area-mussels.

3. Bono, Laura. "The FCC Just Approved 6 GHz Frequency Band for Wi-Fi and Why You Shouldn't Use It." *Children's Health Defense*, November 20, 2020. https://children-shealthdefense.org/news/the-fcc-just-approved-6-ghz-fre-quency-band-for-wi-fi-and-why-you-shouldnt-use-it/; Naren, Anubhav Elhence, Vinay Chamola, and Mohsen Guizani. "Notice of Retraction: Electromagnetic Radiation Due to Cellular, Wi-Fi and Bluetooth Technologies: How Safe Are We?" *IEEE Access* 8 (2020): 42,980–43,000. https://doi.org/10.1109/access.2020.2976434.

Chapter 11

1. "Exercise Boosts Blood Flow to the Brain, Study Finds," March 23, 2021. https://www.utsouthwestern.edu/news-room/articles/year-2021/exercise-boosts-blood-flow-to-the-brain.html.

Chapter 12

1. Medic, Goran, Micheline Wille, and Michiel E. H. Hemels. "Short- and Long-Term Health Consequences of Sleep Disruption." *Nature and Science of Sleep* Volume 9 (May 1, 2017): 151–61. https://doi.org/10.2147/nss.s134864.

2. Hablitz, Lauren M. "The Glymphatic System: A Novel Component of Fundamental Neurobiology." *The Journal of Neuroscience* 41, no. 37 (September 15, 2021): 7698–7711. https://doi.org/10.1523/jneurosci.0619-21.2021.

3. Medic, Willie, and Hemels. "Sleep Disruption," 151–61.

4. Medic, Willie, and Hemels. "Sleep Disruption," 151–61.

5. Tempesta, Daniela, Valentina Socci, Luigi De Gennaro, and Michele Ferrara. "Sleep and Emotional Processing." *Sleep*

Medicine Reviews 40 (August 1, 2018): 183–95. https://doi.
org/10.1016/j.smrv.2017.12.005.

ABOUT THE AUTHOR

Tina's work focuses on bringing light to our emotions to heal our health. She teaches through the lens of an acupuncturist, registered herbalist, and through her biology education, but most of all through her life experience. Through her emotional suffering she has opened to truth and wants to share her knowledge to help others know that peace is available to everyone. Visit Tina online at tinadematteo.com.

www.ingramcontent.com/pod-product-compliance
Lightning Source LLC
Chambersburg PA
CBHW020227130626
46549CB00005B/1770